THE BIOHACKING ENTREPRENEUR

THE BIOHACKING ENTREPRENEUR

Copyright 2025 © Wendi Blum Weiss & Patricia Wooster

All information, techniques, ideas and concepts contained within this publication are of the nature of general comment only and are not in any way recommended as individual advice. The intent is to offer a variety of information to provide a wider range of choices now and in the future, recognizing that we all have widely diverse circumstances and viewpoints. Should any reader choose to make use of the information contained herein, this is their decision, and the contributors (and their companies), authors and publishers do not assume any responsibilities whatsoever under any condition or circumstances. It is recommended that the reader obtain their own independent advice.

WoosterMedia LLC
Tampa, Florida
woostermediabooks.com

ISBN: 979-8-9861607-9-5

The moral right of Wendi Blum Weiss & Patricia Wooster as the author of this work has been asserted by them in accordance with the Copyrights, Designs and Patents Act of 1988.

Published by WoosterMedia LLC
woostermediabooks.com

WoosterMedia

TABLE OF CONTENTS

Introduction 1

CHAPTER 1: Biostacking for Peak Performance: Your Brain, Business, and Body by Wendi Blum Weiss 7

CHAPTER 2: Trust Your Body's Intuition by Patricia Wooster 25

CHAPTER 3: Resilience, Reinvention, and the Legacy of Hank Asher by Lacey Asher 39

CHAPTER 4: Failing Forward: The Hidden Biohack by Kate Beck 53

CHAPTER 5: Biohacking My Way to a Healthier Life and Financial Freedom by Kathy Binner 67

CHAPTER 6: Biohacking Vitality: The Blueprint for Mind-Body Transformation Through Innovative Technology and Personalized Care by Leila Centner 85

CHAPTER 7: Make Yourself Harder to Kill: Biohacking the Central Nervous System for a Solid Foundation of Healing By Dr. Rocco Crapis 103

CHAPTER 8: The Healing Power of Connection: A Biohack for Mental Health by Eileen Lemelman 119

CHAPTER 9: My Story: A Journey to Owning Wellness by Sandra Salce 135

CHAPTER 10: What Does Your Gut Instinct Say?
by Jawna Standish 151

CHAPTER 11: From Prada Heels to Muck Boots
by Andrea Wanerstrand 175

Conclusion 195
About the Authors 197
Thank You (leave a review) 201

INTRODUCTION

Dear Wellness Advocate:

If you're holding this book in your hands, chances are you're not someone who settles. You're ambitious. You're driven. You understand that success in business doesn't just come from strategy, sales, or hard work. It comes from optimizing *yourself*.

We live in a world where burnout is celebrated, sleepless nights are seen as a badge of honor, and caffeine-fueled hustling is considered the key to success. But what if we told you there's another way? What if we told you that your greatest business advantage isn't just in your skills or knowledge but in your health, your energy, and your ability to perform at your peak every single day?

Welcome to the world of **biohacking**, the ultimate game-changer for entrepreneurs.

The Intersection of Health and High Performance

We, Wendi and Patricia, have walked the path of high-achieving entrepreneurs. We've built businesses, navigated challenges, and learned firsthand that no amount of financial success can replace the need for mental clarity, physical vitality, and emotional resilience.

Entrepreneurship is demanding. It tests you at every level. But here's the secret. You don't have to choose between success and well-being. You can have both. In fact, your business will thrive because you prioritize your health.

Biohacking isn't about extremes or gimmicks. It's about understanding your body, making small, intentional changes, and stacking healthy habits that create exponential results over time. Biohacking is about working smarter, not harder, whether it's optimizing your sleep, fueling your body with the right nutrition, reducing stress, or enhancing cognitive performance.

A New Way to Approach Success

Inside this book, you'll find stories, insights, and strategies from entrepreneurs, who have learned how to integrate biohacking into their daily lives. Some came to biohacking out of necessity, pushed to the edge by stress, illness, or exhaustion. Others discovered it as a tool to unlock their full potential. No matter how they got here, they all share one thing in common. They made the choice to take control of their health, and in doing so, transformed their lives and businesses.

This book will introduce you to

- How small, consistent biohacks can dramatically improve your energy, focus, and productivity
- The link between peak performance and optimal health and how to harness it for success

- Real-life experiences from entrepreneurs who have used biohacking to elevate their business and well-being
- Tools, techniques, and cutting-edge research that you can start implementing today

We're not here to tell you to overhaul your entire life overnight. We know you're busy, and we know change can feel overwhelming. But what if **one simple shift**—one tweak to your morning routine, one shift in your mindset, one better habit—could completely change how you show up in your business and life?

Your Health Is Your Business Strategy

We spent years chasing success, only to realize that without health, there is no wealth. When you're constantly tired, stressed, and running on empty, you're not just hurting yourself. You're limiting your impact. You are your company's greatest asset. Taking care of yourself isn't a luxury; it's a necessity.

Think about the most successful entrepreneurs in the world. They don't just work hard. They optimize their bodies, their minds, and their environments. These entrepreneurs prioritize movement, sleep, nutrition, mental clarity, and stress management because they understand one truth: Success is a direct reflection of how well you take care of yourself.

The Time Is Now

We challenge you to go into this book with an open mind. Some biohacks will resonate with you, and others may not. That's okay. The goal isn't to try everything; it's finding what works for you.

- Start small
- Stay curious
- Experiment

Where could you have more energy? More clarity? More focus? How would your business and life change if you felt unstoppable every single day?

This book is your invitation to find out.

We're honored to share this journey with you. By the time you reach the final page, we hope you feel empowered to take control of your health, unlock your full potential, and build a business that thrives because you do.

Here's to your success, your well-being, and your limitless potential.

Wendi Blum Weiss & Patricia Wooster

THE PROCESS OF BIOHACKING, REINVENTING YOURSELF, SHARING YOUR EXPERTISE, AND AMPLIFYING YOUR VOICE ISN'T JUST FOR A SELECT FEW. IT'S FOR ANYONE WHO IS WILLING TO TAKE THE FIRST STEP.

Wendi Blum Weiss

CHAPTER 1

BIOSTACKING FOR PEAK PERFORMANCE: YOUR BRAIN, BUSINESS, AND BODY
BY WENDI BLUM WEISS

There's a unique kind of tension in a medical waiting room. It's not just the people waiting to see their doctor—it's the collective unease that hangs in the air, a quiet, unspoken understanding that no one truly wants to be there.

To this day, I can still envision the despair in those patients' eyes.

My health journey was sparked by a desire to get on the proactive side of medicine. Back in the day, I worked for a major pharmaceutical company, calling on doctors, hospitals, and clinics. The training was intense. Every drug I launched, from antivirals for HIV and hepatitis B to cardiovascular medications, required a thorough knowledge of its clinical trials and research—including the side effects and the unexpected power of the placebo effect.

This reinforced my desire to *steer clear* of meds at all costs. It made me highly aware of **the importance of**

prioritizing my health because I saw the reverse side of it for twenty-five years. It set me on a purposeful path toward a holistic lifestyle. I began with meditation and breathwork.

Meditation didn't come easy—I spent six months noticing nothing, hiding in my closet while meditating so my family wouldn't think I was a weirdo. But over time, subtle shifts emerged, and one day, I had a transcendent experience, as if I had ascended beyond time, space, and what we know as reality. The sense of peace and freedom fascinated me. Shortly thereafter, I researched what happened and discovered neuroplasticity (the science behind reprogramming the subconscious mind).

Breathwork followed: a simple practice of inhaling for four counts, holding for four, exhaling for four, and holding the exhale. It quickly calmed my nervous system by dialing down the sympathetic nervous system (sometimes referred to as the fight-or-flight response) and activating the parasympathetic nervous system (also known as the rest and digest state). Fifteen years later, both practices remain part of my daily routine.

My curiosity was so intrigued that I became obsessed with learning the science behind these wellness practices. I took trainings and became certified in neuro-linguistic programming (NLP), which I discovered was the basis for Tony Robbins' seminars and teachings. I also acquired additional training in EFT, hypnotherapy, Reiki, and other modalities.

The revelation I experienced through learning all these new modalities not only enhanced my personal well-being but also led to a major decision to change careers. I decided, after twenty-five years, to resign from my position in pharma, but they convinced me to stay on with them part-time. I continued to call on a few of our major accounts, one being the hepatology division of the University of Miami, and one of the top doctors started referring patients to me. Ironically, he referred to me as "the female version of Tony Robbins."

My First Client

I'll never forget my first client. She had spent three weeks in the hospital due to a near-fatal alcohol-induced cirrhosis of the liver.

Before our first session, I pulled into her driveway and sat in my car for fifteen minutes, setting intentions and hoping (actually, *praying*) that I could help her in some meaningful way. When she finally opened the door, I was taken aback.

Based on what the referring doctor had told me about her case, her sex, her age, her diagnosis, and her current clinical condition, I expected someone who looked scruffy and worn out from the ordeal she'd been through. Instead, she looked like a beautiful angel.

She asked, "What were you doing in my driveway for so long?" When I explained that I had been setting my intentions for our session, her entire demeanor softened.

I entered, expecting to find a house in disarray. Instead, I found beautiful art on the walls and her bird singing softly in the background. I asked her about the paintings on the walls, and she humbly mentioned that she had painted them herself. Not only was she the opposite of what I'd expected, but she was also a gifted artist.

I realized I had unfairly stereotyped this woman, and I had been completely wrong. This stunning woman filled with grace was suffering from loneliness and a lost sense of purpose. Drinking wasn't the root cause—feeling hopeless was.

We deeply connected as she shared with me her story of her unmet dreams, hopes, and desires, and her personal loss. I knew we needed to start slowly. I introduced to her the first few simple steps: **taking a walk outside and getting fresh air, simple breathwork, and a five-minute meditation.** That's it. Nothing complicated.

Four weeks later, after doing the work consistently, she began to feel like her old self again. She even pulled out a line of baby clothing she had created years prior and asked me to help her relaunch it. It was miraculous to witness her transforming with the same simple biohacking tools I used a decade earlier. We don't know what we don't know until we know it. She was a perfect example of this.

My Healing Journey: How I Discovered Biohacking

I was a type A personality, always hustling to make ends meet as a single mom, but my life was stressful. My upbringing had been rough, with a lot of drama I had to navigate. Over the years, despite having a successful career and the outward appearance that I had everything under control, I was secretly spinning out of control, struggling with low self-esteem, panic attacks, and even suicidal thoughts.

For years, I equated health only with working out—I had that part down. But the issue for me wasn't physical; it was psychological. Training the mind is as important as training the body. Investing time equally between mind and body. In the same way that we can reshape the body through physical fitness, we can remodel the brain through various mindset methodologies, such as the **REMM biohacking framework** (more on this later).

What was interesting to me was the research around the mind-body connection in every area of our lives, including our careers. Staying in a job you hate negatively affects your physical body almost as bad as smoking cigarettes or abusing alcohol. Stress, dissatisfaction, and emotional discord take a toll on your health in ways you might not even realize. The same is true for staying in relationships that drain your energy. Stuck energy doesn't just trap you emotionally—it manifests physically, impacting your body, mind, and spirit.

Too many people have it backward—and I was almost one of them. Most people wait for the perfect moment to pursue their dreams. It takes a lot of courage to reinvent yourself, but I turned in my resignation at fifty and am living proof that it's never too late.

Through these modalities, anything and everything is possible. It all begins with the power of a thought.

You're never stuck, although it may feel that way. Thoughts become tangible things, and when you change your thoughts, you can change your career and your entire life.

The Accumulation Effect: Biostacking One Tool at a Time

The changes in my life didn't end there. I felt a pull—an undeniable calling—to **help others live healthier, more intentional lives**, too. I couldn't ignore the voice inside me saying, *"This is not enough. There is more you can do."*

Today, I dedicate my life to empowering others not just to think differently about their health, habits, and mindset, but to share their unique stories, messages, and expertise with the world. I believe that when we give our voice to our experience and wisdom, we can inspire others to make choices that lead to a healthier, more vibrant life.

As I continued to embrace holistic practices for myself, I began exploring ways to stack these small changes, leading to what we now call "biostacking."

For me, biostacking is about making small, intentional changes that add up over time—changes that stick and truly make a difference. I'm proud to say that fifteen years after embarking on this journey, at sixty-four years old, I am still medication-free and learning how to stay that way with more tools every single day. The following is just a snapshot of what that looks like in my everyday life.

INTRODUCTION

My Mornings: Biohacking for Peak Performance

Each morning, I wake up at 5 a.m., brush my teeth, and head straight to the kitchen for two glasses of **alkaline water with electrolytes**. Five years ago, I finally convinced my husband to install an alkaline water system. He thought I was going overboard, but now that he's done more reading on the subject, he sees the benefit. After that, I make a quick protein shake, buckle on my weight belt, and head out the door for **a brisk walk**. There's something about moving my body out in nature that clears my head and sets the tone for the day ahead.

By 8 a.m., my creative energy is at its peak. I like to start my days with **the hardest, most creative work first**—stuff that requires my full attention, like writing, creating slides for speeches, analyzing projects, and any other priorities—before diving into calls and meetings. By late morning, I'm usually attending events, networking, returning calls, on Zoom with coaching clients, or leading a class or session for our author community. I feel very fortunate to love what I do and have the great honor of working with smart and talented people.

Our energy waxes and wanes throughout the day. To optimize my performance, I **take frequent breaks**. Between calls, I jump on my rebounder or vibration plate, both of which currently sit in plain sight in our dining room. I also put on my headset, play upbeat music, and probably look like a crazy person as I dance around the house.

I use **red light therapy** several times a week as an energy booster to help maintain my stamina. And yes, I drink coffee (decaffeinated), usually a latte in the morning and another one later in the day. One of these days, I may consider cutting back on my coffee addiction, but not today!

Nighttime Routine: 8:30 Wind Down

At 8:30 p.m., I start my winding down routine. For years, I would go to bed feeling the pressure of the day and would occasionally wake up in the middle of the night. There were several times when I could feel my heart racing prior to the onset of a panic attack. From time to time, I would also have a disturbing nightmare that left me feeling exhausted and emotionally drained the next day. It was a cycle I couldn't seem to break. My life improved when I made a conscious decision to create a nighttime routine. These days, my sleep is seldom interrupted, and I'm grateful to wake up feeling calm, rested, and looking forward to conquering the day.

My evening routine begins with a moment to **review my calendar** for the following day. I mentally walk through what's coming up—meetings, tasks, or events. Knowing what's ahead gives me a sense of control and helps me go to bed with a clear mind. From there, I soak in a tub of **Epsom salts**. There's something so calming about warm water that signals my body and mind to relax. This step alone has been a great ritual for a reset right before sleep.

INTRODUCTION

Part of my routine includes **reflecting on the day's wins**. They don't have to be monumental. It could be as simple as having a productive meeting or carving out time for a workout. Just as important, I release any lingering upsets or negative emotions. I've learned not to carry any negative baggage into bed with me. You'll be in bed for the next six to eight hours, so it's very important to wipe the slate clean, setting the stage for a good day tomorrow.

Next, I focus on **three things I'm grateful for**. I don't write these down; I just think about them. Gratitude is such a powerful practice, and it doesn't have to be complicated. Sometimes, I'm grateful for small moments like a meaningful conversation with a friend. Because sleep takes you into a higher brain wave state, focusing on gratitude before falling asleep helps you have a peaceful night's rest.

I also throw in **visualization** and reverse engineering something I want to create. Whether it's a health goal or a new project for my business, this practice energizes me into the future. The thoughts we think just before going to sleep at night go deepest into our subconscious mind.

Tracking is important, and these days, we have many wearable devices to give us metrics, including sleep data. I use my Oura ring to track my sleep, my heart rate, my stress level, and other readiness measurements. With these insights, I've been able to refine my habits and prioritize rest in a way that's most useful for me.

I've named a lot of things here, but there are nights when I only hit 30% of them, but even at that, it makes a significant difference (and it's more than the majority of the population). When I take care of my nights, my days take care of themselves.

How to Create Your Biostacking Routine

When I look back, it's clear how little shifts in routine have changed my life, allowing me to show up as my best self every day. My journey through biohacking didn't happen overnight. "Progress over perfection" is my mantra.

I slowly add one new habit each quarter, giving myself time to build consistency. For me, it's about quality over quantity—there's no point in piling on too many changes that won't stick. By focusing on one thing at a time, I optimize my health, my relationships, and my business without feeling overwhelmed.

Take a moment to **reflect on your routine**. Where does your energy dip or your focus waver? What small tweaks could help you infuse more energy, joy, or productivity into your day?

Biostacking isn't about being perfect. Some days, I don't hit every step in my routine, and that's totally okay. What matters is commitment, small steps, and striving for consistency over time. Keep in mind that small habits compounded daily eventually create big results.

What is the "why" behind what you do?

For much of my life, I struggled with insecurity. Moving often as a teenager meant constantly starting over at new schools, always feeling like an outsider. Even now, I continue to work on my sense of self-worth and self-esteem. But along the way, I discovered powerful tools for confidence building and owning my power—tools that I now use to help others write their books and speak on stages with confidence and self-worth. I want to help others discover the same thing for themselves.

Today, through our book writing programs, cohort designs, and speaking opportunities, Patricia Wooster—my business partner and most amazing bestie friend—and I guide our clients to create a lasting impact while building their personal and professional legacies to help them amplify their voices and impact. Together, we create a ripple effect of transformation—making the world a place where people live longer, feel happier, and thrive.

If you want to write a book, change your career, or reinvent yourself at any age, you can. I made the leap at fifty-three, and I've never looked back. If I can do it, so can you.

What unique framework or service do you offer to your community or clients?

The framework Patricia and I offer is designed to amplify voices and transform lives by helping people step into their purpose and share their expertise. Our programs aren't just about writing a book or giving a speech—they're about helping clients discover their unique story, refine their message, and share it in a way that resonates deeply with their audience. We help clients overcome self-doubt, find clarity, and step confidently into their role as thought leaders.

One of my favorite success stories is Susan, a 60-something therapist with a thriving practice. She joined one of our co-author book projects after starting a successful podcast, but like many others, she struggled with self-doubt. "Who am I to write a book?" she asked herself. Susan also had a difficult history—she'd been burned before by another company that made big promises about helping her write a book but never delivered.

What makes our framework unique is the strong sense of community we foster. Weekly meetings, hands-on coaching, and a network of like-minded authors ensure that no one feels alone. Susan embraced the process, and now, two co-author books later, she has written her own book. This year, she is the keynote speaker for a large conference, has built a thriving community, and continues to expand her influence.

What's even more rewarding is that many of our authors, like Susan, go on to write books after contributing to our projects. About 25% of our clients continue working with us on multiple books or cohort programs.

Community is at the heart of everything you do. Writing and speaking can feel isolating, but with our support, clients join a collaborative environment where they feel seen, heard, and supported every step of the way. Together, we celebrate wins, navigate challenges, and create meaningful, lasting change—not just for our clients but for the people their stories touch.

Our mission is simple: to give people the tools, the confidence, and the platform to share their voice with the world in a way that makes a profound impact on their audience, their business, and their lives.

The Best Professional Tip or Advice I've Received

You are worthy.

You are worth far more than you think you are. You are worthy of excellent health, outstanding relationships, and the freedom to be wealthy and financially secure.

Here's the truth: You can **reinvent yourself** up to your very last breath. It's never too late, and you always have something valuable to offer the world. Your voice matters. Your story matters. You are a masterpiece, and you must take precious care of yourself.

No one is coming to save you. It's up to you to grow your discipline muscles, be impeccable with the promises you make to yourself, and honor your worth every single day. Don't shortchange yourself.

Life goes by in a flash. **Don't compromise**. You deserve a rich, beautiful, healthy, and fulfilling life.

What's your favorite biohack?

The year before I turned in my initial resignation from my career in pharma, I created a happiness survey. I stacked them on a clipboard and went out and asked people to rate their happiness on a scale of one to ten, with many of the questions based on their career. The answers quickly reflected the quality of their lives. Across the board, those who were happier at work were happier in life overall, and those who were unhappy at work seemed to always struggle.

I thought about those surveys a lot back then. I always felt like I was missing something, and the surveys were confirming what I already knew in my heart of hearts. Although my career was good to me, I always felt there was something more. The research I was doing with my happiness questionnaire reinforced my decision to segue into a new profession. I decided to trust my intuition and switch careers even though I didn't know what it would look like.

Earlier, I referred to the REMM biohacking framework, which stands for Reverse Engineering Mindset Mapping System. This was a system I put together organically as I was searching for a way to reinvent myself.

It's as if life is a jigsaw puzzle, and somehow we have to put the pieces together to direct us to our next stage of life. First, I had to know what I didn't want: to be stuck in a career I was unsure about for the duration of my life. Second, was how to reprogram my mind to believe I could make a change this late in life. Third, I needed role models, like Louise Hay of Hay House Publishing, who became a publisher in her 50s and modeled what that could look like for me. Fourth, I had to script out in vivid detail a brand-new story for my life calling. And lastly, I had to own my power and self-worth. Earlier, when I referred to the REMM biohacking framework, that was the formula I organically put together to reinvent myself, recognizing what I needed to change my career and life completely.

Over the last fifteen years, I have used this process, and 75% of what I have REMMed has happened almost verbatim to how I visualized, recorded, and energized around it. In 2014, I REMMed seeing an entire table of my books in Barnes and Noble in the front of the store as I did a book signing, to marrying my soulmate in a spiritual, Bali-type wedding, to having an amazing grandson that I adore.

I have used this process to REMM my partnership with Patricia—I actualized this by using my REMM framework. Most importantly, I have taught and used the same process with hundreds of clients.

I could probably write an entire book on the REMM system and its profound results. It's a combination of writing, speaking, recording, and listening to voice recordings repeatedly until they become ingrained in your belief system and motivate you to act on your goals, dreams, and desires.

For now, I'll just say that I truly believe this process saved my soul and my life, and I am grateful for the opportunity to share it with others.

Closing Thoughts: Your Story, Your Legacy

Biohacking isn't for everybody, and that's the beauty of it. With an entire arsenal of tools *stacked* to fit what works best for you, you can develop a routine that is literally life-changing.

Everything I've shared—my journey, the tools I use, REMM, and the frameworks I teach—is built on one belief: **You are capable of extraordinary transformation.** Your story matters. Your voice matters. And the choices you make today have the power to create a ripple effect that extends far beyond you.

The process of biohacking, reinventing yourself, sharing your expertise, and amplifying your voice isn't just for a select few. It's for anyone who is willing to take the first step. Whether it's writing a book, rethinking your health, or stepping into your purpose, the key is to start.

The tools are here; the support is here, and the time is now. Your journey starts with a single decision: to believe in your worth, take control of your narrative, and create a life that is vibrant, fulfilling, and impactful.

These days, I wake up feeling grateful to God to be here, thankful for my husband, my two sons, and my grandson, and fortunate to be living the life I've created. If I can do it, you can, too.

The world is waiting for your story.

How can people connect with you?

I can be found at WendiBlum.com and LinkedIn @WendiBlum.

CONSISTENCY IN MY HABITS AND ROUTINES, WITH AN EMPHASIS ON PREVENTION, IS WHERE I STAY FOCUSED.

Patricia Wooster

CHAPTER 2

TRUST YOUR BODY'S INTUITION
BY PATRICIA WOOSTER

panic [*pan-ik*]

1. To experience extreme fear because you cannot remove your foot from your car's gas pedal—particularly when your three-year-old and six-month-old sons are in the backseat.

Panic is exactly what I felt when my car jumped the curb and I lost control. It's the day my brain stopped communicating with my feet. I was in my son's preschool parking lot. It was six months before I got behind the wheel again.

My physician's first educated guess for the tingling in my hands and feet was multiple sclerosis. The first stop for diagnosis was an MRI brain scan. It was "inconclusive," a word I often heard for the next twenty-one years. Next, came the spinal tap. That procedure sent me to the emergency room twice, and I lost 10 pounds in 10 days. Inconclusive.

My doctor referred me to the top MS doctor in the region, which did not instill a ton of confidence in me given the ambiguous interpretation of "inconclusive" in my medical reports. For several months, my schedule became a rotation of specialists and pharmaceuticals. Every weekday morning, my parents showed up, one to watch the boys and the other to chauffeur me to a new appointment. Over the years, my medical records would show possible diagnoses of multiple sclerosis, brain tumors, rheumatoid arthritis, lupus, Crohn's, central sensitivity syndrome, chronic fatigue, neuropathy, and many others I can no longer remember.

In between these various tests and doctors is a lot of waiting. And with waiting comes worry. Chronic illness is not meant for the impatient (which I am) as it comes with uncertainty and symptom management as you navigate the healthcare system. Each new appointment starts with hope and often ends with more question marks.

In 2013, my annual lab work showed low levels of ferritin. This VIP protein stores iron in your cells and releases it when needed. It protects you from iron deficiencies or overload. My doctor shrugged it off, but I was meticulous about my medical details, so I asked for a referral to a hematologist. This would not be the last time where self-efficacy served me well.

When you see a hematologist, the first thing they do is run their own labs. So, although I had my latest lab report, they collected blood for real-time analysis. My specialist's first question to me was, "Who drove you here?" When I answered that I drove myself, I saw him raise his eyebrows to the nurse.

He replied, "Your ferritin level isn't even registering on our test. You don't have any, and a normal level is 1500. I can't figure out how you are awake."

Ethically, he wouldn't let me leave without a two-hour iron infusion, which started three years of infusions in a chemo center. Some of those infusions lasted six hours. I was scoped in every direction, trying to find the source of my blood loss, but every test came up empty. My next stop was the Mayo Clinic. And after days of tests and a whole-body workup, I heard my favorite word again, "inconclusive."

At the same time, I became very active at the gym. Pushing my body to extremes was fuel for my soul. I ran 5Ks, saw a personal trainer, and ate organic nutritious foods. If my body was going to ache and tingle anyway, then at least I would be in shape. My parents feared I was pushing too much, but what it did for my mental health was priceless.

I read every book I could on mindfulness. I became obsessed with the concept of "thoughts became things." With ferritin levels so low for so long, neuropathy became a permanent repercussion, which caused the tingling in my hands and feet. By changing my thoughts, I could tune out the tingling, which is a practice I have to this day. Now, whenever I get sick or anxious, the tingling returns—proof that it still exists.

In 2016, I was in my best physical shape when the dominos fell differently. It started with a new symptom—a 90-day migraine. I called upon my Rolodex of specialists and tried every prescription in the book, from pills. I.V. drips to injections and steroids. I even had a balloon sinuplasty to remove a few sinus polyps to see if that helped. Nothing worked.

Six months passed, and I woke up with a twinge in my back. I thought it was a pinched nerve from playing tennis. I popped a few ibuprofen, applied a heating pad, and waited for it to heal. A few days later, I noticed a funny cough-like sound every time I bent over. I didn't think much of it, but went to urgent care, hoping for a prescription for my back. Instead, I got a room full of nurses and a doctor rushing into the exam room after my X-ray. She told my husband to drive me straight to the emergency room. I heard the words "spontaneous pneumothorax" but did not know what it meant.

I googled it while my husband drove. I figured I must have misheard because my search results said it was a lung collapse. I was breathing just fine, so thought it was a mistake.

I arrived at the hospital with my left lung over 80% collapsed; it is life-threatening if it is 100%. Due to my cardio through tennis and running, I didn't have symptoms of distressed breathing. I spent a week at the hospital and was told it was a fluke. According to my pulmonologist, it had no correlation with any of my other health problems, and it would probably never happen again.

Until it did. Every month at the same time, I felt the familiar pressure. I tracked it on my calendar and proudly diagnosed myself with catamenial pneumothorax (meaning hormone-driven). My pulmonologist confirmed my WebMD diagnosis, and I was his first patient with this rare disease, so he sent me to a cardiothoracic surgeon.

Three months before my forty-fourth birthday, I had major lung surgery. Picture someone sandpapering your entire lung with the intent of creating maximum inflammation. That's what happened. The scar tissue superglues your lung into your rib cage. If it sounds fun, it isn't. I found out the day after the surgery that it's the second most painful surgery and recovery a person can have. I received multiple blood transfusions and spent eight days in the hospital with three tubes sticking out of my back.

I didn't leave my house for months. And I have zero recollection of Christmas that year. I vaguely remember creating some high school curriculum for my soon-to-be-released book *Ignite Your Spark* with Simon & Schuster, but that's about it. The whole year is a bit of a blur.

And then it stopped. No more collapses—no more migraines. Except for seven days every month (during menses), I was relatively pain-free. The lung pressure I felt in those days (without a collapse) indicated the surgery worked.

But I wasn't done yet.

During Covid, on came skin issues, gastrointestinal problems, esophageal pain, and those damn migraines again. I became allergic to gluten, nuts, and dairy after never having a food allergy in my life. It felt like every day I was eliminating a new food group. In addition, my sense of smell was through the roof. Any hint of cologne, cleaning products, or anything scented sent me to a dark room with a migraine.

I'd had enough. My rotating dance card of specialists wasn't working. I knew there had to be some connection between these random health issues that kept occurring. And I was determined to find out.

What do you do when your body attacks itself, when your symptoms are a constantly moving target, and no one can figure it out?

I picked up a book that changed my life. It is *Forever Young* by Dr Mark Hyman, one of the most prestigious functional medicine doctors at the Cleveland Clinic. His integration of nutrition, physical activity, and mindfulness with traditional medicine interested me. But what really got me hooked was his practice of searching for the root cause of an illness and how it interrelates with various symptoms. No one had taken the time to do that for me yet. My other doctors were masking symptoms with prescriptions.

Luckily, one of his trainees had a practice in my city. And I found hope. My first appointment lasted four hours, and we just talked. They took a detailed medical history of my life going back to when I was in my mother's womb. Things I had forgotten came up, like when my mom found me as a two-year-old chugging a bottle of turpentine, and I had to have my stomach pumped. Or the years of childhood emotional trauma and the stomach problems I had in my teens. Every mental, physical, and emotional corner of my life came up.

Next, I went for lab work, where they collected nineteen vials of my blood. It was super extensive and expensive. And after fourteen years, I heard for the very first time, "Conclusive. We know why you've had these symptoms and problems."

Mycotoxin poisoning, aka mold exposure.

I suspect it happened in our first home, where we had a terrible leak. The timing lines up with my symptoms. These seemingly unrelated symptoms were my body's inability to flush toxins out of my body fast enough.

This is how it was explained to me, and it makes a lot of sense. Think of a big bowl sitting in your gut. Throughout the day, it fills up with toxins and other things your body needs to get rid of. Your body flushes them out so you don't get sick, inflammation, or any other unusual symptoms. But if your body cannot keep up, then it overflows. This is when your body starts throwing a tantrum. It can affect anything from hair loss to autoimmune and sickness.

The goal is to help your body empty that bowl—it's something everyone should be practicing. My baseline is higher due to mold exposure, so my road to recovery is longer, but most of what I am doing would help many people with ailments. We all have bowls in our belly to control and prevent from overflowing.

The greatest gift that comes with having a diagnosis is peace of mind. That's why we have to be our best advocates. No one knows our body like we do, so it's imperative that we don't give up before we have answers. At the same time, you need a community because no one directly understands how you are feeling, whether conclusive or not yet. I've found several private Facebook groups that provided so much comfort during my journey. Know that if you are seeking medical answers for yourself or someone you love, you are not alone.

What is the "why" behind what you do?

It's hard to persevere when you have a chronic illness. I have such empathy for those who do. I know what it feels like when the people around you keep saying to see one more doctor, while you want to give up.

My boys were ages two and a newborn when my medical problems started, so my "why" was bigger than me. It was all about them. I did not want them to grow up in a home where everything revolved around "mommy being sick." Most of the time, they had no idea what was going on. They found out something was happening when my lung collapsed. That year, I spent eighteen nights in the hospital, so it was impossible to hide.

The passion and purpose I find in my business are what have always gotten me from one day to the next. I know that if I help someone achieve their dream, then selfishly, it fills my cup, too. Every day, I work with the most interesting and brilliant people and help them bring their stories to life. My sons are now eighteen and twenty and more generous, kind, and amazing than I could have ever imagined. I've been with my husband and best friend for twenty-eight years, so in every way, I am blessed.

How have you pivoted your business in the last few years?

I am a busy person, but that busyness often leads to being overwhelmed and anxious. I am 100% aware that I do it to myself. Previously, I said "yes" to anyone and everyone. And saying "yes" and people pleasing gets you nowhere. Your availability leads to being taken advantage of, disappointment when you do say "no," and no time to do your best work.

My focus now is energy management. This starts with how I manage my time. Each day is time blocked and themed. Client work on certain days. Deep thinking about others. It allows me to streamline, so I am not context switching throughout the day. It's a work in progress.

In addition, I am sharing my boundaries with others. It's one thing to create them and another to really enforce them. Everyone thinks they are the exception. This year is when I'm keeping score. People who do not respect my time or time off are not supporting my need for self-care. It's hugely disrespectful when we project our agenda, needs, or unpreparedness on other people. I feel that holding my boundaries in place will lead to my greatest business breakthrough of my career.

What role do collaboration and community have in your business?

Collaboration and community are the only ways I want to do business right now. I've been an entrepreneur for twenty years and the first half of my career was struggling to figure everything out. I took so many online courses, coaching programs, and classes on top of weeks and weeks down learning rabbit holes. And then I woke up one day and realized that my time was being spent in tech and admin—two things that I am not very good at.

So to save a dollar, I was losing time. Time I could have spent making money doing what I love. Now, I partner with people with skill sets and geniuses that complement mine. It's a win-win. Each of us gets to focus on the things we love most while still accomplishing what needs to get done. This shows up in my life in many ways:

- Business partnership: Wendi Weiss and I cofounded Mindset to Millions. We share the same values, but have different areas of expertise. We have a fun, supportive, ever-evolving collaborative partnership that creates space for a personal and professional life.
- Client community: Our Unleash Academy is the nurturing space I've wanted my entire career. Our clients are brilliant (and our friends), so

we created a container to learn, grow, and scale together. Whenever I have a question, it's typically answered within this network.
- Community partners: These are businesses we trust to take care of us and our clients. Whether it's products or services, we love to partner with people who are best at what they do.
- Networking communities and events: Everyone needs to surround themselves with people who are pursuing big dreams. It's a matter of curating an environment rich with inspiration and empowerment. It's easy to get stuck at home behind a computer, so these experiences expose us to new ideas.

What is your favorite biohack and why?

Two things have contributed to my quality of life and well-being the most. Consistency in my habits and routines, with an emphasis on prevention, is where I stay focused. My biggest advice is to try many things and find what works best for you. One of my former clients is not a morning person. His afternoon routine closely mirrors what I do when I wake up. Follow your body's natural preference, and you'll notice a huge difference.

1. Strong Morning Routine

My favorite biohack is my morning routine. I wake up every day around 5:30 a.m. without an alarm and spend the first hour reading, journaling, and easing into my day. Then, depending on the day (and weather), I either take an hour-long walk or go to the gym for a combination of cardio and weight training.

After a workout, I spend twenty minutes in my HigherDOSE infrared blanket, meditating and detoxing my body. Next, I drink a special smoothie recipe from my doctor. It's a gut reset blend combined with various minerals and vitamins I need in my system. In addition, it includes collagen, probiotics, and blueberries. When I am on top of my program (some days I fall off), I take twenty supplements and use a binder to remove biofilm and the toxin burden on my body. Removing the mycotoxins from my body is a work in progress.

My entire routine on a weekday lasts about 2 ½ hours and are the most productive hours of my day. It increases my energy and sets my intentions for the day. It's where my most creative ideas always originate.

2. Functional Medical Doctor

A functional doctor approaches healthcare by identifying and addressing the root causes of health issues rather than just treating symptoms. They view the body as an interconnected system while considering how different aspects of your lifestyle, environment, and genetics impact your overall health. It's invaluable when you have a variety of symptoms but no diagnosis.

Working with a functional doctor often involves comprehensive testing, in-depth consultations, and personalized treatment plans. They can help with chronic conditions like fatigue, autoimmune disorders, hormonal imbalances, or gut health issues by uncovering underlying factors such as nutritional deficiencies, inflammation, or stress. My team includes a doctor, nutritionist, and holistic pharmacologist.

What I find most valuable is that they empower you to take an active role in your health. They emphasize prevention, personalized care, and long-term wellness rather than quick fixes. Treatment does not start with Band-Aids and symptom maskers. It's often a combination of supplements, food, mindfulness, and health technology. They look at the treatment and prevention options and create a plan that focuses on prevention, wellness, and your overall well-being.

How can people connect with you?

I can be found at woostermediabooks.com and on LinkedIn @PatriciaWooster.

I'VE LEARNED THAT LIFE IS A SERIES OF REINVENTIONS, EACH ONE REQUIRING A UNIQUE BLEND OF STRENGTH, CREATIVITY, AND DETERMINATION.

Lacey Asher

CHAPTER 3

RESILIENCE, REINVENTION, AND THE LEGACY OF HANK ASHER BY LACEY ASHER

The first time I stepped onto the taekwondo mat, I could barely tie my belt. But by the age of twelve, I stood at the edge of the mat in the final round of the Junior Olympics, my heart pounding in rhythm with my breath. It wasn't just any competition; it was the culmination of years of relentless training, discipline, and determination. My second-degree black belt was tied tightly around my waist, a symbol of all that I had endured. The hours of drills, bruises, and late-night workouts flashed through my mind, but none of that mattered in that moment. What mattered was the opponent standing across from me and the victory within reach. I walked away with two bronze medals for the U.S. Girls Junior Olympics Taekwondo team. Though I felt a slight pang of disappointment for not bringing home the gold, I was proud not to leave empty-handed.

But my life wasn't always defined by victory. Shortly after the Olympics, at just thirteen years old, I discovered

I was going to be a mother. This revelation turned my world upside down and led me to the Harkins Home, a shelter for pregnant women. Uncertainty and struggle marked my days and nights. Yet, I remained resilient, holding on to the belief that this was a temporary phase. The challenges, though overwhelming at times, shaped my tenacity, preparing me for the life ahead.

As my story continued, my life took another sharp turn. At twenty-two, I met Hank Asher—a man whose legacy would forever change mine. Known as the father of data fusion, Hank was a force of nature. His technology revolutionized the way law enforcement tracked criminals, creating tools that saved countless lives. But Hank wasn't just a tech pioneer; he was deeply committed to humanitarian work, particularly in Haiti. From constructing schools to delivering essential supplies to rebuilding communities devastated by natural disasters, Hank's efforts were both profound and personal.

Being a part of Hank's mission was an honor I still carry with me. I had the privilege of witnessing and contributing to his groundbreaking work firsthand. Whether it was helping to develop advanced technologies or participating in humanitarian efforts, each day with Hank filled me with purpose. One of the most transformative experiences was our time in Haiti. We didn't just deliver aid, we helped rebuild lives. Hank's hands-on approach, from assembling resources to overseeing construction, was a testament to his dedication. Seeing the direct impact of his work inspired me to contribute more deeply to the causes I cared about.

As our bond grew, Hank became more than a mentor—he became family. When he faced the heartbreak of a failed adoption attempt, I tried to offer comfort. I told him, "I think it would be an honor to be an Asher." His response was immediate. With a smile, he called his attorney and said, "Change Lacey Greenroad to Lacey Asher." Months later, it became official, and he granted me the honor of carrying his name. It was a profound moment for me, one that validated my place in his world and strengthened my resolve to carry on his legacy.

The last four years of Hank's life were both deeply rewarding and heartbreakingly difficult. During that time, I stayed by his side, especially during the holidays, when many others had walked away. Those moments, filled with both joy and sorrow, remain etched in my memory. Losing Hank was devastating. I saw him just the day before he passed, and he seemed fine. His absence left a void that I struggled to fill. For a time, I turned to alcohol to cope, but one morning, I woke up and realized this wasn't how my story would end. Determined to honor Hank's memory, I began the slow process of rebuilding my life.

I returned to my roots in health and fitness, finding solace in the discipline of training. The gym became my sanctuary, a place where I could channel my grief and rediscover my strength. This renewed focus led me to the racing community—a passion I had nurtured since childhood. I built my rally car and participated in the

Gold Rush Rally, reigniting a spark that had long been dormant.

Racing became more than a sport; it became a platform for philanthropy. I used my success to raise funds for causes close to my heart, including the Wounded Warrior Foundation. One of my proudest moments came when I was named first runner-up out of 35,000 women in the U.S. for Maxim Magazine, raising significant funds for the foundation. During this time, I also earned my SCCA racing license and competed in Formula 4, marking a high point in my career.

But just as my racing journey was reaching new heights, COVID-19 struck. The pandemic canceled my first championship in Monterey, Mexico, effectively ending my racing career. It was a difficult loss, but I chose to see it as an opportunity to pivot once again. I immersed myself in yoga and meditation, finding both physical and mental rejuvenation. These practices became cornerstones of my daily life, helping me maintain clarity and resilience. Yoga and meditation aren't just hobbies; they're essential biohacks that keep me grounded and energized, allowing me to navigate life's challenges with grace.

My passion for biohacking also led me to discover SkinKick, a revolutionary skincare product that has transformed my life. As someone who struggled with severe acne growing up, finding an all-natural, non-toxic solution felt like a miracle. SkinKick is more than just a product; it's a testament to the power of clean, effective skincare. It's the one product I recommend to everyone, and I'm proud to share my love for it through my work.

Another game-changer in my biohacking journey has been methylene blue. This powerful compound has become a staple in my health routine, offering incredible benefits for cognitive function and overall well-being. Combined with my commitment to yoga, meditation, and other biohacks, it's helped me stay sharp, focused, and resilient.

Today, I've channeled my experiences into new ventures, including The Product BuzZ, my podcast on YouTube. Through this platform, I interview people with innovative products, brands, and services, sharing their stories with the world. It's a labor of love that combines my passion for entrepreneurship with my commitment to helping others succeed.

As I look back on my journey, I see a tapestry woven with resilience, reinvention, and purpose. Every triumph and challenge—taekwondo, motherhood, racing, philanthropy, and now The Product BuzZ—has been shaped by my commitment to growth. I've learned that life is a series of reinventions, each one requiring a unique blend of strength, creativity, and determination.

And through it all, biohacking has been my anchor. Whether it's the clarity from yoga and meditation, the healing powers of SkinKick, or the cognitive boost from methylene blue, these tools have allowed me to keep moving forward, no matter what life throws my way. As I prepare to contribute my story to a biohacking book,

I hope to inspire others to explore the ways they can optimize their lives.

Ultimately, my story is a tribute to the legacy of Hank Asher and the resilience of the human spirit. With each new chapter, I strive to honor his memory while creating my own, proving that even in the face of profound loss, we can find purpose, strength, and joy.

What is the "why" behind what you do?

My journey stems from a deep passion to inspire others because I've been through a lot in my life. Growing up, I had a very rough childhood, and it took me a long time to get to where I am today. I came from a homeless shelter and, at one point, didn't even have enough money for food or clothes. I didn't have a car and was navigating life as a teen mom. But I never gave up. I always believed in myself, even when the odds were stacked against me.

This experience gave me immense compassion and a determination to help others. I want people to see that no matter where you come from or what your circumstances are, you can overcome challenges and achieve your dreams. That's why I'm so passionate about supporting others who are in situations similar to where I once was. I want to be a source of hope and empowerment, particularly for young women and teen moms who might feel like their dreams are out of reach.

To me, this is more than just a mission—it's a calling. I actively give back through charitable work because I understand firsthand what it's like to be in need. My story is a testament to the fact that your circumstances don't define you. If you keep fighting and believe in yourself, you can create the life you want. That's the message I want to leave for others: You are capable, and your dreams don't end just because life throws you challenges. You've got this.

How have you pivoted your business in the last few years?

My journey in business has involved significant pivots. I started out as an athlete, fully dedicated to martial arts, boxing, and racing. For years, my athletic career was my entire world. But over time, my body started telling me it was time to slow down—it wasn't something I could ignore. I'm not twenty-one anymore and continuing in the same way just wasn't possible. That realization forced me to step back and rethink my future. I needed to find a new path where I could channel my passion, share my experiences, and continue making a positive impact.

That's when I decided to transition into podcasting, and *The Product BuzZ* was born. Podcasting gives me a platform to connect with others meaningfully while offering them the exposure I was fortunate to gain during my athletic career. Through *The Product BuzZ* podcast, I bring captivating stories to life. It's a space filled with thought-provoking interviews, engaging storytelling, and an exciting mix of topics. The podcast serves as a gateway to new perspectives and meaningful discussions, offering something for everyone—whether you're seeking personal growth, entertainment, or a moment of escape.

I also use my social media channels to amplify these conversations, extending the reach of these stories to inspire as many people as possible. On the podcast, we explore the magical world of products—the good, the bad, and the ugly—while uncovering the creativity and passion behind them. It's about creating a community of curiosity and discovery, where listeners can tune in, let their imaginations soar, and find inspiration in unexpected places.

Although I've retired from my athletic career, my mission has remained the same: to empower and uplift others. I've learned that pivoting doesn't mean giving up; it means evolving and finding new ways to share your passion. I'm excited to continue this adventure, helping others unlock their potential and sharing stories that truly matter.

What advice would you give to someone considering entrepreneurship?

My advice to anyone considering entrepreneurship is to make sure you are deeply passionate about the path you choose. When you become an entrepreneur, your business becomes your life. It's not just a job; it's something you live, eat, breathe, and sleep. Everything in your life will revolve around it, and you need to be ready and willing to make sacrifices. These sacrifices are hard to fully understand until you're in the thick of it, but they are an inevitable part of the journey.

The key is to put your heart and soul into what you do. If you're truly committed, your efforts will eventually pay off. But the most important thing I can say is this: never, ever give up—no matter what. I've fallen on my face more times than I can count. I've faced setbacks, challenges, and moments where it felt like everything was working against me. But each time, I've dusted myself off and told myself, "Today is a new day." Perseverance is everything because you never know when your breakthrough is just around the corner.

For me, that one life-changing opportunity came in the form of Hank. If I had given up while living in a homeless shelter, I would never have met him. That experience taught me that no matter how dark things may seem, there is always hope and potential for something incredible to happen. So my advice is simple: stay passionate, work hard, and never stop believing in yourself and your dreams. That next opportunity might be closer than you think.

What is your favorite biohack and why?

My favorite biohack, hands down, is methylene blue. A lot of people haven't heard of it, and its history is so fascinating. Back in the 1920s, it was used to treat malaria and even to dye blue jeans—which always surprises people. They hear that and think, "Why would something used on fabric be good for humans?" But let me tell you, the benefits are absolutely incredible.

Methylene blue is an amazing nootropic, which means it helps enhance brain function. Studies have shown that, even at low doses, it improves mitochondrial efficiency—how your cells produce energy. This translates into clearer thinking, better focus, and sharper memory. It's like giving your brain a little boost of energy. For me, it was a game-changer. The very first time I tried it, I felt the difference immediately. I'm talking clarity, focus, and just an overall feeling of being on top of my game—not in seven days, not in thirty days, but right then and there.

What's even better is that methylene blue has been linked to mood enhancement. It works by increasing levels of neurotransmitters like serotonin and norepinephrine, which can alleviate depression. That's one reason I love it so much—it doesn't just give you mental clarity; it also uplifts your mood, making you feel balanced and energized.

On top of that, it's a powerful anti-aging tool. It has antioxidant properties that help neutralize free radicals and reduce oxidative stress, which means it protects your cells from damage and supports overall health. I think of it as one of those underrated biohacks that more people need to know about. Here are some different applications:

1. **Boost Brain Power**
    - Methylene blue supercharges your mitochondria (hello, cellular energy!) by donating electrons in the energy production process.

- Research shows low doses can enhance memory and cognitive performance, making it your new best friend for productivity hacks.

2. **Protect Your Brain for the Long Haul**
   - This compound is like a shield for your neurons, reducing oxidative stress and keeping your brain sharp.
   - Studies suggest MB could prevent tau protein buildup—key in fighting Alzheimer's and other neurodegenerative conditions.

3. **Defy Aging**
   - Mitochondria age as you do, but MB says, "Not today!" It powers up your cells, reduces oxidative damage, and slows down the clock.
   - Research even shows it supports healthier, younger-looking skin by boosting collagen production and cell vitality.

4. **Level Up Energy & Endurance**
   - Feel unstoppable! By enhancing oxygen utilization and ATP production, MB can help fight fatigue and improve athletic performance.

5. **Glowing Skin & Faster Healing**
   - Want radiant skin and quick recovery from cuts or scrapes? MB promotes collagen production and supports wound healing.

6. **Natural Defense Mechanism**
   - MB isn't just about performance; it's a germ fighter too. Its antimicrobial properties can

help tackle tough infections (bonus: it's even been used to treat malaria!).

I'm always experimenting with new things, but methylene blue is something I keep coming back to. It's a secret weapon of mine that makes me feel amazing, and I'd love to see more people give it a try. It's such a versatile and effective biohack, and I truly believe it has the potential to help so many people live healthier, sharper, and happier lives. Like anything, do your research and consult an expert before putting anything new into your body.

How can people connect with you?

I can be found at laceyasher.com and on YouTube @TheProductBuzz.

WHEN WE LIVE AND LEAD WITH PURPOSE, EMPOWERMENT, ACCOUNTABILITY, AND RESILIENCE, WE LEAVE BEHIND A LEGACY THAT STANDS THE TEST OF TIME.

Kate Beck

CHAPTER 4

FAILING FORWARD: THE HIDDEN BIOHACK BY KATE BECK

From an early age, people described me as precocious—a trait that would shape my journey in unexpected ways. At ten years old, I orchestrated my mother's marriage by calling up my friend's father and inviting him to dinner, even writing out the menu myself. This innate drive to create positive change would become both my greatest strength and, at times, my blind spot.

Growing up in a loving but financially modest family, I learned early that there was always enough—enough for the stray dog, the stray kid—and always work if you wanted it. While we didn't have brand-name luxuries, we had abundance in spirit. This foundation would prove crucial in my later years, though I wouldn't realize it until I had lost everything. Twice.

My entrepreneurial journey began conventionally enough. Through determination and natural ability, I built a successful insurance practice. By my early thirties, I had it all—a thriving business, a beach house, commercial real estate, even an airplane. I was living what many would consider the epitome of success. But I had overlooked something fundamental: self-advocacy and protection.

In a devastating turn of events, I lost everything practically overnight. My marriage ended, and with it went the beach house, the commercial property, everything I had built. The worst part? I had made a classic entrepreneur's mistake—I hadn't protected myself with proper contracts. My business, my client relationships, everything I had built was legally tied to others. When those relationships ended, so did my access to what I had created.

Most people would consider this a once-in-a-lifetime lesson. I had to learn it twice.

After rebuilding from my first loss, I found myself in a similar situation with a new firm. I was making excellent money, writing millions in premiums, winning customer service awards. But once again, I had failed to secure proper contracts. When the promised partnership didn't materialize, I was let go, losing my entire book of business—again. The month I was fired, I was supposed to make $26,000 in commissions. Instead, I had to start over from scratch.

I still remember lying on my floor, screaming in frustration. I had hit my target number, and achieved what I thought was success, only to watch it vanish—again. But this time was different. This time, I had reached my turning point.

With support from my new partner and his family, I made the decisive choice to start over—differently. We cut all expenses, moved in with family, and I launched my Medicare insurance brand. I started with just 20 clients when I needed 500 to make a living. But this time, I was building on a foundation of self-advocacy and protection.

Why Medicare? Because it's necessary. With 10,000 people turning 65 every day until 2065, there's a consistent need for guidance through this complex transition. But more importantly, I had finally found a way to combine my natural inclination to help others with a sustainable business model that I controlled.

The journey taught me several crucial lessons about personal and professional biohacking:

1. Self-Advocacy Is Non-Negotiable
   - Your success must be built on a foundation of proper protection.
   - Legal contracts aren't just paperwork; they're your safety net.
   - Being good at what you do isn't enough; you must also be good at protecting what you build.

2. Clean Slate Thinking
   - Sometimes starting over is your greatest opportunity.
   - Failure isn't final unless you stop trying.
   - Each restart is a chance to build better systems.

3. Sustainable Success Requires Balance
   - Rapid growth without proper foundation leads to collapse.
   - True success includes both professional achievement and personal well-being.
   - Your business should support your life, not consume it.

4. Energy Management Is Critical
   - Surrounding yourself with the right people is crucial.
   - Sometimes you need to remove people from your life to grow.
   - The brighter and more balanced you are, the more you attract bright and balanced people.

These lessons fundamentally changed how I approach business and life. They led me to explore frameworks like positive intelligence and to understand that true biohacking isn't just about optimizing our physical health; it's about creating sustainable systems for success in all areas of life.

Today, I run a successful Medicare insurance practice, but more importantly, I've built it in a way that aligns with my values and protects my interests. I've learned that the real measure of success isn't just in the numbers; it's in creating a sustainable, balanced life that can weather any storm.

My journey taught me that the most important form of biohacking isn't found in supplements or optimization techniques; it's in learning to advocate for yourself while staying true to your values. It's about building systems that support your growth while protecting what you've built. Most importantly, it's about creating a life that's not just successful by external measures, but sustainable and fulfilling on your terms.

What is the "why" behind what you do?

My deepest motivation stems from a desire to help people see beyond their current challenges and into the opportunities they present. Growing up, I witnessed two contrasting family environments: one filled with joy despite limited means and another consumed by negativity despite material comfort. This stark contrast showed me how mindset and emotional well-being can profoundly impact our lives, regardless of external circumstances.

I've seen too many people, including family members, get stuck in their pain, unable to see past their current challenges. They become trapped in what I call the "itchy sweater," a state of discomfort that's easier to endure because it's familiar, even though shedding it could reveal opportunities for growth and transformation. My mission is to help people plant what I call "purposeful, empowering gardens"—sustainable systems and mindsets that support long-term well-being. Through this process of heart gardening, we plant seeds of peace and nurture growth that leads to lasting transformation.

This mission manifests in two ways. First, through my Medicare insurance practice, I help people navigate one of life's significant transitions with clarity and confidence. But beyond that, I'm passionate about sharing the lessons I've learned about sustainable success and emotional well-being. Because true health—the kind that lets you live vibrantly to a hundred and beyond—isn't just about physical wellness. It's about creating harmony between your personal values, professional endeavors, and emotional well-being.

How were you able to transform a setback into a setup for success?

My biggest transformation came after losing everything for the second time. Here's how I turned that setback into lasting success:

1. Acceptance and Assessment
   Instead of dwelling in victim mode, I took full responsibility for my situation. I had to acknowledge that while others' actions hurt me, my lack of proper business protection allowed it to happen.

2. Strategic Downsizing
   I made the difficult decision to dramatically simplify my life—moving in with family, cutting expenses, and starting with just twenty clients. This wasn't a step backward; it was creating a proper foundation.

3. Building Better Systems
   This time, I built my business differently:
   - Proper contracts and business structures from day one
   - Clear boundaries and expectations in all relationships
   - Focus on sustainable growth over quick wins
4. Maintaining Perspective
   I learned to view success differently. Instead of chasing numbers, I focused on
   - Building genuine, protected business relationships
   - Creating sustainable systems for growth
   - Maintaining work-life balance
   - Ensuring my business serves my life, not the other way around

What life or business lessons have created the most growth for you?

The most profound growth in my life has come from what initially appeared to be devastating setbacks. Here are the key lessons that transformed my journey:

1. Trust Must Be Verified
   The most expensive lesson I learned—twice—was that handshake deals and verbal promises aren't enough in business. No matter how much you trust someone or how well things are going, every business relationship needs proper documentation

and protection. This isn't about distrust; it's about professional respect and clarity.

2. Your Business Model Matters More Than Your Effort
Early in my career, I believed that working harder was the answer to everything. I learned that choosing the right business model is far more important than how many hours you work. Medicare insurance isn't the most glamorous field, but it's necessary and sustainable. This taught me to prioritize practicality over prestige.

3. The Power of Starting Over
Learning to start over—not just once, but twice—taught me that what seems like an ending can be your greatest beginning. Each time I lost everything, I gained something invaluable: clarity about what really matters and how to build more sustainably.

What has been your ultimate life lesson?

Perhaps the most important lesson I've learned is that true success isn't about avoiding failures; it's about failing forward. Each setback has the potential to teach you exactly what you need to learn for your next level of growth. The key is to stay curious, maintain perspective, and remember that every challenge is an opportunity to build something better.

In biohacking, this mindset is crucial. Just as we optimize our physical health through incremental improvements and systematic changes, we can "hack" our path to success by learning from setbacks and building better systems. The goal isn't perfection; it's progress and sustainability.

Remember: Your journey is your greatest teacher. Every setback, every failure, every moment of doubt—these are all opportunities to build something stronger, wiser, and more sustainable. Embrace them, learn from them, and use them to create a life and business that can truly stand the test of time.

Bonus Memo: The Timeless Power of Values

If I could add one more reflection, it would be about what makes someone or something truly timeless. For me, the answer lies in values—the guiding principles that shape our actions, decisions, and legacy. In my life, I refer to these as my *Pearls of Wisdom*: purpose, empowerment, accountability, and resilience.

These values are more than just ideals; they are a compass, helping me navigate challenges and opportunities alike. By leading my life with these values, I not only create a foundation for sustainable success but also plant seeds of peace—both personally and professionally. Every interaction, every decision, every step forward is an opportunity to sow these seeds and nurture their growth.

This, my dear friends, is what I believe makes a life or endeavor timeless. It's not about perfection or external accolades but about the enduring impact we create through our values. When we live and lead with purpose, empowerment, accountability, and resilience, we leave behind a legacy that stands the test of time.

And that, above all, is the essence of being timeless.

What advice would you give to someone considering entrepreneurship?

If you're considering entrepreneurship, here's what I wish someone had told me:

1. Choose Necessary Over Exciting
   - Look for what people need, not just what excites you
   - Build a business that serves a clear, ongoing market demand
   - Consider the sustainability of your chosen field

2. Protect Yourself First
   - Get everything in writing
   - Invest in proper legal and business structures from the start
   - Don't let excitement or trust override proper business practices

3. Build Sustainable Systems
   - Create processes that can weather personal and professional storms and re-assess them annually

- Focus on steady growth over rapid expansion
- When you feel stuck, ask yourself: What's the smallest step I can take toward progress?

What is your favorite biohack and why?

My favorite biohack might seem surprisingly simple, but it's profoundly effective: using physical organization as a tool for mental and emotional clarity. When I'm feeling heavy or stuck, unable to identify what's bothering me, I start with something tangible—cleaning my car, organizing a drawer, or decluttering my pantry.

This practice works on multiple levels:

1. Immediate Tangible Results
   - You can see and feel the progress.
   - It provides a sense of accomplishment.
   - It creates physical space that reflects mental clarity.

2. Emotional Processing
   - The methodical nature of organizing allows your mind to process underlying thoughts.
   - Physical movement helps release emotional tension.
   - Creating order externally helps create order internally.

3. Sustainable Impact
   - Organized spaces reduce daily stress.
   - Clear environments promote clear thinking.
   - Regular maintenance becomes a meditation practice.

The beauty of this biohack is its accessibility and compound benefits. Anyone can do it. It costs nothing but time, and the benefits extend far beyond the physical space you're organizing. It's a practical way to implement what I call "planting seeds of peace"—creating small, manageable changes that grow into lasting positive impact.

Sometimes, the most profound changes in health, wealth, love, and happiness begin with the smallest, unrelated steps. Unnoticed thoughts, feelings, and habits that quietly take a toll often weigh our lives down. Where else in your personal life could you fit in a healthier choice?

For me, it starts each morning with something simple: water mixed with two teaspoons of chlorophyll and spearmint, followed by waiting two hours to enjoy a caffeinated hot beverage. When I share this with clients or colleagues, they often say it seems too simple to make an impact. Yet, the most transformative biohacks are often the most straightforward. Just as I help clients navigate the complexities of Medicare by simplifying decisions, these seemingly minor actions create momentum. They clear space, both mentally and emotionally, for purposeful choices that ripple into every corner of life.

How can people connect with you?

I can be found at https://www.timeless-vitality.com/ or on LinkedIn @katebeck.

FREESTYLE LIVING IS ABOUT FREEDOM—FREEDOM TO SPEND YOUR TIME HOW YOU WANT, FREEDOM TO FOCUS ON THE THINGS THAT TRULY MATTER, AND FREEDOM TO LIVE WITHOUT THE CONSTANT STRESS OF CHASING THE NEXT DOLLAR.

Kathy Binner

CHAPTER 5

BIOHACKING MY WAY TO A HEALTHIER LIFE AND FINANCIAL FREEDOM BY KATHY BINNER

For as long as I can remember, I've been hustling. But today, the hustle looks a lot different. I'm no longer caught up in the rat race, grinding to survive. No, I've finally found that sweet spot where I'm making money and living my best life in terms of health, freedom, and happiness. And let me tell you, getting here wasn't easy. It took a lot of work, some huge risks, and a complete shift in how I approached my life.

Right now, I'm in a place where I can honestly say I have the best of both worlds. I've built a steady stream of passive income through real estate and my online international academy, allowing me to focus on what matters: staying healthy, spending time with loved ones, and most important, enjoying the life I've worked so hard to build. But the road to this point? It wasn't all sunshine and smooth sailing. It was a rollercoaster, filled with struggles, sleepless nights, and, at times, doubt.

Looking back, it's amazing to see how far I've come. There's no longer a need for me to chase money to the point of exhaustion. Instead, I've found a way to let money work for me. And furthermore, I've learned that health has to come first, no matter what. It wasn't until I found this balance between health and wealth that I finally felt like I was truly living.

The Early Hustle: Single Mom Life

Let's rewind for a second. I was a single mom, trying to make ends meet with two minimum wage jobs. Trust me, there's nothing glamorous about the hustle when you're living paycheck to paycheck, constantly worried about how you'll keep the lights on. The stress was *real*. It was a constant companion, whispering in my ear whenever the rent was due or the car needed repairs. There were nights I'd lie awake, wondering how to stretch my next paycheck to cover groceries, gas, and daycare.

I remember this one night when things felt like they were spiraling. My car had broken down, and I had no cash to fix it. I worked back-to-back shifts at a hotel, managing a team by day and slinging banquets by night. It felt like no matter how much I worked, I could never get ahead. I'd drive home in my beat-up car (once it finally got fixed) after an exhausting shift, just to crash for a few hours before waking up to do it all over again. I was always tired—mentally, physically, emotionally. But there was no option to slow down. There was no safety net. If something went wrong, the entire house of cards would come crashing down.

That pressure, that constant fear of failure, was what motivated me to find a way out. I knew I couldn't keep living like that. I needed to take control of my life, and the only way to do that was by finding a skill that could give me real financial independence. That's when I realized my nail tech was making more income by doing nails than what I was making working my multiple corporate jobs. I researched a nails-only program at a local cosmetology school, and everything changed.

The Nail Tech Lifeline: A Bigger Dream

Signing up for the nail tech program was a leap of faith. I didn't know anything about doing nails, but I knew I needed to make a change and make more money. This felt like my shot. Becoming a nail tech wasn't just another job; it was a way out of the cycle of low-wage work. It meant I could finally control my income, set my schedule, and create a better future for myself and my kid. So, even though I was already working crazy hours, I signed up.

Cosmetology school was no walk in the park. Sometimes I'd come straight from my stressful corporate day job to my evening class, trying to stay alert while learning how to sculpt acrylic sets of nails, do pedicures, and apply polish. But I was determined. I knew that every lesson and every skill I learned was a step closer to breaking free from the grind. And the more I learned, the more I saw the possibilities. I wasn't just getting a certification; I was building a path to freedom.

When I finally graduated and attained my license, it felt like I had this new superpower. I could now work for myself, make more money, and most importantly, see the growth potential. Becoming a nail tech wasn't the end goal; it was just the beginning of a much bigger dream.

The Salon Experience: Working for Others and Craving Freedom

After earning my license, I landed a job in a local salon, and at first, it was everything I'd hoped it would be. There was this energy in the salon, a kind of buzz that made every day exciting. I was building a steady client base, finally making enough money to pay the bills without panicking every month. But the more time I spent there, the more I realized that while I had a bit more control over my life, I still wasn't where I wanted to be.

The salon work was intense. Working twelve-hour days, dealing with difficult clients, and trying to be the best acrylic girl in the city was taking its toll. There were days when I'd leave the salon so exhausted I could barely drive home. And even though I was technically making more money, it felt like I was trading one kind of stress for another.

Even though I dreaded the thought of having *all* the responsibility, I knew I couldn't keep working for someone else forever. I needed more financial stability and more control—not just over my schedule, but over my finances. That's when I started dreaming about opening my very own salon.

Opening My Salon: The Power Play

So I took the plunge. With everything I had saved—and trust me, it wasn't much—I partnered with another nail tech to open our salon. That was the real power move. If I was going to break free from the grind, I had to have more control over the finances. However, the dream of owning a salon wasn't just about making more money; it was about finally being in control of my time, my income, and my life.

The early days of running the salon were *wild*. I was learning on the job, managing not just the clients but also the staff, the bills, the inventory, you name it. There were days when I wondered if I had bitten off more than I could chew. I'd get a call from a stylist saying they couldn't come in last minute, or the electricity would go out right before a big booking. Every day was a new crisis, but at the same time, every day was a new lesson.

I'll never forget this one incident that pushed me. A client had booked a wedding party—one of those big, lucrative deals—and we were short-staffed because one of my stylists decided to call off at the last minute. I remember thinking, "This is it. Either we pull through or we lose a big client." So I jumped in. I did nails, helped with hair, and even made coffee for the bridal party. It was chaos, but we made it through, and that moment showed me I had what it took to handle anything.

Despite the stress, owning the salon was empowering. I was no longer answering to someone else. And every time a client walked out with a smile or I saw the books in the black, it felt like all the hard work was paying off.

But the more the salon succeeded, the more it demanded of me. And the irony? The very freedom I had worked so hard for started slipping away. Instead of working for someone else, I was working for the salon—the stress was *next level*. My health took a hit, and that's when I realized something had to change. I had built a successful business, but at what cost? It wasn't just about financial freedom anymore; I needed to get my health back on track.

Real Estate: The Pivot to Wealth

As the salon grew, I began thinking about what would come next. I didn't want to be trapped behind a nail table forever, no matter how successful the salon became. I had this gut feeling that real estate was the key to building *real* wealth—the kind of wealth that would give me both financial freedom *and* freedom over my time.

It started with the building my salon was in. Instead of continuing to rent, I made the bold decision to buy a commercial building. Owning the building meant that I could turn the rent I had been paying into an investment, and it also meant I was taking my first real step into real estate.

At first, I didn't know what I was doing. I had no experience in commercial real estate, but I dove in headfirst. The numbers made sense, and owning the property felt like leveling up. I wasn't just a salon owner; I was now a real estate investor. And that changed everything.

I started educating myself on how real estate worked, and the more I learned, the more I saw the potential. Commercial real estate was just the beginning. I realized I could apply the same principles to residential real estate. That's when Marc and I started buying houses. We'd buy run-down properties, fix them up, and rent them. It wasn't glamorous work, but the returns were undeniable.

Rehabbing houses wasn't easy; it was *gritty*, especially at first. There were weekends spent knocking down walls, painting rooms, and dealing with plumbing disasters. But every rehab taught us something new, and the rewards kept getting bigger. Soon, we weren't just rehabbing houses; we were building a portfolio of rental properties. And with each new property came passive income—*the holy grail* of financial freedom.

The beauty of real estate is that it creates a snowball effect. Once you have a few properties generating passive income, it gives you the freedom to reinvest and keep growing your wealth. I went from being stressed out over rent to owning multiple properties that paid me every month. That's when I started to breathe a little easier.

Building the Real Estate Empire: Neglecting My Health

Our real estate journey didn't stop there. After a few successful rehabs and a growing rental portfolio, Marc and I started thinking bigger. We weren't just dabbling in real estate anymore; we were building our little empire. We started looking for multi-family units, properties that could generate even more income without adding a ton of extra work.

The first multi-family property we bought was a game-changer. It was a small four unit, but it was big enough to provide us with multiple income streams from just one investment. Managing it came with its set of challenges, from dealing with tenants to maintaining the property, but the payoff was worth it.

With each new property, I saw how much power there was in owning real estate. The passive income gave us the flexibility to take more risks and make bigger moves. And it wasn't just about the money anymore; it was about freedom. Freedom to spend more time with family, to travel, to focus on my health. That's when I realized that financial success wasn't just about having money in the bank; it was about using that money to buy back my time.

But as we built our real estate empire, something else became clear: while I had figured out how to build wealth, I had been neglecting something just as important—my health.

The Dalai Lama Moment: Realizing Health Comes First

It was around this time that I had what I now call my "Dalai Lama moment." I had spent years grinding to build financial security, but I had ignored the most important thing—*my health*. The turning point came when I read a quote from the Dalai Lama. It hit me like a ton of bricks. He said, "Man sacrifices his health to make money. Then he sacrifices money to recuperate his health." And let me tell you, I felt that on a *deep* level. I had spent years building financial freedom, but I was running on fumes, neglecting my body, and dealing with the physical toll of years of stress and long hours.

That quote made me stop in my tracks. I had worked hard to create a life of freedom, but what good was all the money, all the success, if I wasn't around to enjoy it? I knew I needed to make a serious change. This wasn't just about losing weight or looking good; it was about getting my life back.

What is the "why" behind what you do?

As I embraced freestyle living, I realized that I wasn't alone on this journey. So many people out there are stuck in the same grind I was in, working themselves to the bone but never really feeling free. That is why I do what I do! They have the money, but they're too stressed, too tired, or too unhealthy to enjoy it.

What unique framework or service do you offer to your community or clients?

That's when I knew I had to share what I had learned. It wasn't enough for me to have figured this out for myself—I wanted to help others do the same. That's why I started the Kathy Binner International Academy, an online platform where I teach others how to find their path to financial freedom and health.

Through my courses, mastermind groups, and one-on-one coaching, I help people build wealth by finding their passion, turning it into their purpose, and finally making it passive. I help them create the kind of life they *want* to live. I teach them the importance of balance—how to hustle without burning out, how to build wealth without sacrificing their health, and how to live on their terms.

How were you able to transform a setback into a setup for success?

That's when I stumbled upon intermittent fasting. I had tried every diet under the sun, from low-carb to calorie counting, but nothing seemed to stick. Fasting, though? It wasn't just another fad. It was a complete shift in how I approached food and my body. It wasn't about deprivation; it was about giving my body the chance to reset and heal.

The more I read about it, the more I was convinced this was the key. Not just for weight loss, but for overall health. Autophagy—the body's natural process of cleaning out damaged cells and regenerating healthier ones—was something that resonated with me. It made sense. By giving my body a break from constantly digesting food, I could heal from the inside out.

I started slowly, easing into intermittent fasting with a 16:8 schedule—16 hours of fasting, and 8 hours of eating. The first few days were rough, I'm not going to lie. I was used to grazing throughout the day, so going without food for that long felt unnatural. But after the first week, something amazing happened. I stopped feeling hungry all the time; my energy levels skyrocketed, and I could *feel* my body getting stronger.

Within a few weeks, I started noticing real changes— my clothes were fitting better; I had more mental clarity, and I was sleeping like a baby. The most surprising part? The chronic aches and pains I had been dealing with for years faded. My gums, which had always been a problem spot, were healing. My skin was clearer, and the brown age spots I had been seeing lightened. It was like my body was thanking me for finally giving it the break it needed.

What role do collaboration and community have in your business?

Collaboration and community have been instrumental in the success of my business journey, particularly as I've shifted from surviving to thriving. As I built my real estate empire and the Kathy Binner International Academy, I quickly realized that achieving success alone wasn't sustainable. It took a community of like-minded people to help me reach new heights, whether it was through sharing knowledge, offering encouragement, or providing expertise that I didn't have myself.

In the realm of real estate, collaboration became essential. Marc and I worked together to build our rental property portfolio, and without his insights and expertise, I would have faced challenges that could have set us back. Our partnership allowed us to capitalize on each other's strengths, with Marc handling the nitty-gritty of repairs and rehab while I focused on property management, financial strategies, and scaling our business. Together, we not only survived but thrived in a competitive market.

The community aspect extended beyond just our team; it was about connecting with other investors, contractors, and even mentors who helped us navigate the real estate landscape. There's a wealth of knowledge that comes from others who've already made the mistakes, learned the lessons, and are willing to share their experiences. This collaborative exchange helped me make more informed decisions, avoid pitfalls, and ultimately scale our business more quickly.

In my online academy, collaboration plays a pivotal role in the success of the members. My academy isn't just about me teaching others; it's about creating an environment where everyone can learn from each other. The members are not just clients; they are part of a network of entrepreneurs, real estate investors, and professionals who can lean on each other for advice, guidance, and support. I've witnessed firsthand how people in the community thrive when they collaborate, whether it's through mastermind groups, mentorship, or sharing a success story that encourages others to keep going.

Community also fosters accountability. As I work toward my health and wealth goals, having others to keep me accountable has been essential. I learned quickly that staying motivated was much easier when I had a support network, whether it was from fellow real estate investors or those I've met through my health journey. By surrounding myself with a community that values both health and wealth, I've been able to make better choices in both areas of my life. Collaboration with others is the secret to scaling not just business but life itself.

The Legacy I Want to Leave: It's About Freedom

Looking back, I realize that everything I've done—every pivot, every struggle, every success—has been building toward this moment. I didn't just want to build a successful business or make a lot of money. I wanted to build a legacy.

The legacy I want to leave isn't just about wealth. It's about teaching others that they don't have to choose between health and wealth—they can have both. It's about showing people that true freedom comes from living life on your terms, not someone else's.

That's the legacy I want to leave. Not just for my family, but for anyone who's ever felt stuck in the grind, trapped by the need to make money at the expense of their health and happiness. Because at the end of the day, it's not about the money; it's about *freedom*. Freedom to be healthy, freedom to be wealthy, and freedom to live the life you've always dreamed of.

The Journey Continues: Here's to Wealth and Most Importantly, Health

And that's the beautiful thing—it's a journey. I'm still learning, growing, and figuring out new ways to live freestyle. But now, I'm doing it on my terms, with my health and my wealth in balance. And I'm excited to see where the journey takes me next.

So here's to the hustle. Here's to building wealth *and* health. And here's to living life on your terms.

What is your favorite biohack and why?

The most powerful and my favorite biohack has been the shift in my mindset. Fasting taught me patience and discipline in a way that nothing else ever has. It isn't just about the food; it is about taking control of my health, setting boundaries, and prioritizing what truly matters.

Health Before Wealth: My New Mantra

That's when I adopted a new philosophy: *Health comes before wealth*. I had been living it backward for so long, putting financial success above everything else. But what good is money if you're not around to enjoy it? That realization shifted everything for me. I started to prioritize my health the way I had once prioritized my business.

I made time for exercise, found ways to reduce stress, and most importantly, started listening to my body. Instead of pushing through exhaustion or ignoring pain, I began to see my health as my most valuable asset. Because here's the truth: you can always make more money, but you can't buy more time. And if you don't have your health, what's the point of all that wealth?

This shift in mindset didn't just improve my physical health; it made me a better business owner and friend. I had more energy to pour into my real estate ventures, and I became more intentional with my time. I wasn't chasing success anymore; I was creating a life I *wanted* to live.

Freestyle Living: Designing a Life on My Terms

The real beauty of finding this balance between health and wealth was that it allowed me to embrace what I now call *freestyle living*. Freestyle living isn't about following someone else's blueprint for success; it's about designing your life on your terms. For me, that meant taking control of my health, my time, and my business in a way that worked for *me*.

Freestyle living is about *freedom*—freedom to spend your time how you want, freedom to focus on the things that truly matter, and freedom to live without the constant stress of chasing the next dollar. It's about knowing when to hustle and when to rest. It's about building wealth, yes, but also about building a life you love.

For me, that meant scaling back on the things that didn't serve me—like spending endless hours at the salon—and focusing more on the things that did, like real estate and my health. It also meant learning to say *no* more often. If something didn't align with my vision for my life, it had to go. I stopped letting other people's expectations dictate my decisions and started living in a way that felt true to who I was and where I wanted to go.

How can people connect with you?

I can be found at www.kathybinner.com and on Instagram @kathybinner

IF YOU'RE NOT PROACTIVELY CREATING YOUR HEALTH JOURNEY, IT'S BEING CREATED FOR YOU.

Leila Centner

CHAPTER 6

BIOHACKING VITALITY: THE BLUEPRINT FOR MIND-BODY TRANSFORMATION THROUGH INNOVATIVE TECHNOLOGY AND PERSONALIZED CARE BY LEILA CENTNER

You never forget the moments that change your life. Those memories stay seared in your consciousness forever, right down to the tiny, seemingly mundane details.

I can see myself now, years ago, standing in the bedroom. My husband and I were business partners (we still are), and he stands in front of me. He has just asked me a simple question, an accounting detail related to our business, and he's waiting for an answer.

It's the sort of question I answer a dozen times a day, recalling facts and figures of our day-to-day operations without fail. But this time, all I can do is look at him blankly and say, "I don't remember."

My husband turns, blinks in surprise, and just stares at me. "What do you mean you don't remember?" he says. "Leila, you remember everything!"

For a few moments, all I can do is stare back at him, unsure of what to say because *I'm* not sure what I mean either! I've always had a sharp memory. It's part of what's gotten me so far in my professional career. But my mind is drawing a blank. It's like my brain isn't working correctly.

A few seconds pass, and my husband is looking at me strangely, no longer amused but almost suspicious, as if he thinks I might be hiding something from him. And who can blame him? Usually, I really *do* recall every detail.

But I truly don't remember—I *can't* remember.

Something isn't right here, I think. *What's going on with me?*

For many months, I've been in denial that anything is wrong. It's not just my memory. Normally, I'm known for being a high-energy person, but I'm constantly fighting fatigue, always feeling like I need another nap. I've noticed that it sometimes feels like my speech starts to slow, like the words won't come and I'm trying to catch up with my thoughts. A host of minor symptoms had been creeping up within me and gradually getting worse, but I'm the type of person who says, "I'm going to power through this."

I told myself that these symptoms weren't a big deal and that I was too busy right now to deal with them. So, instead of addressing the issue, I just kept rolling with the punches. I acted like everything was fine. I tried to hide the truth from my husband, from myself, and from the rest of the world until it was the right time to address it.

The sad irony is that a few years prior to this, I had stood next to my brother as he lay in a hospital bed after years of trying to hide the pain of living with unmanaged diabetes, convinced that he didn't need to address it. Maybe he thought he could ignore the problem and move on. I remember wondering what on earth he had been thinking to let himself get this bad.

"Promise me that you'll never do this again," I remember telling him. "Your body is trying to tell you something. Don't ignore the signs. When you're not feeling right, you need to get help. Promise me that you'll take care of yourself and you'll tell me."

"I promise," he said.

But six months later, it was the same thing all over again.

In the end, my brother passed away after going to great lengths to hide his health issues. And now, here *I* was, doing the same thing, behaving as if I could ignore my body's check engine light until it was the right time to address it.

At that moment, I realized that I needed to make the same promise to myself that I'd urged my brother to make to me: to never ignore the signs, to prioritize my health, and to take ownership of my health. This would require bold, decisive action to change not only my physical conditions and circumstances but my entire mindset about my health.

There was just one problem... Where do I start?

First, I needed to understand what was happening within me. Second, I had to strengthen myself and detox from it. And finally, I had to develop a new path forward. If I could find a system that would do all that, I could create a future of optimal vitality for myself.

Little did I know that over the course of the next few years spent traveling the world, meeting healers, learning about every type of therapy and modality you can imagine—and making a few costly and painful mistakes along the way—my promise to myself would lead me to *build* the very system I was searching for. It would also lead me to create the largest biohacking and integrated medical center in the world, dedicated to personalized care through innovative technology and holistic healing.

What is the "why" behind what you do?

Maybe you, like me, have also found yourself waiting for the right time to address one or multiple symptoms. Maybe you tell yourself it's not a big deal. But it's time to get honest with yourself. It *is* a big deal. And by putting it off, what you're really doing is neglecting your health.

My worldwide search for answers was a quest to get back to the way I was before—my old normal. I discovered a few nasty surprises, including Lyme disease, mold, parasites, and a whole array of toxins I had never even heard of. Even more shocking, I learned that in today's world, practically *all of us* have these dangers brewing within our bodies, and most of us never even know it.

No matter what your individual case may be, one thing is certain: *If you're not proactively creating your health journey, it's being created for you.* And if you're headed down the wrong path like I was, your body will send you increasingly painful messages to get you to listen.

An array of biohacking modalities and deep changes got me healthy, and my mindset on health shifted so much that I was far above my old normal, and I never wanted to go back.

Today, I am the CEO of Centner Wellness and Spa, Miami's premier destination for wellness and biohacking, currently serving four locations. Since opening in 2024, we've helped people get back in control of their health and their lives with the world's largest collection of biohacking technologies and integrated medical resources, all under one roof. We offer everything from hyperbaric chambers for oxygen therapy and healing to Ammortal Chambers for rejuvenating at the cellular level, theta chamber therapy for deep mental relaxation and recovery, extracorporeal blood oxygenation and ozonation protocol (EBO2), IV therapies for detoxification and revitalization, and much more.

We go deeper than any other facility in the world. And we do so through a comprehensive blueprint that has helped thousands of people learn how to heal every aspect of their bodies.

I believe your journey to recovering your health does not have to be lonely, painful, or disjointed. In fact, with a strategic plan, your path to biohacking your vitality can be pleasant, clear, and lasting.

What is your favorite biohack and why?

At Centner Wellness, our innovative treatments support bio-optimization through detoxification, cellular regeneration, enhanced neurocognitive function, stress reduction, and decreasing inflammation—everything you need to feel whole again.

Just as every individual is unique, so are the health challenges they face. So, how do we help our clients biohack their way to wellness? Based on exhaustive research and experience, we have developed a step-by-step pathway leading from chronic illness to optimal vitality, transitioning clients from poisoned to vital.

The **Vitality Blueprint** follows three crucial steps:

1. **Assess**
2. **Strengthen and Detox**
3. **Revitalize and Recharge**

Step 1: Assess

When it comes to health and vitality, your source of power lies in a solid base of understanding. After all, how can you heal without knowing what's really going on inside you?

One of my favorite things about our **Assess** phase is that we don't just take labs. We reach deep to search for the underlying root cause of issues. Is it heavy metals, parasites, mold, or infection? Is it something spiritual or energetic? We assess all this at a depth that most clinics, even functional clinics, miss during first-level testing.

We have assessments that measure biochemistry, brain, body, and bioenergetic processes. Most other clinics only measure one or two of these assessments and rarely have the medical providers with the expertise to incorporate, understand, or interpret all the various aspects of assessing health and longevity potential.

A doctor or provider is usually only trained in one or two specialties. In the best-case scenario, each practitioner will give you a tiny piece of the puzzle that may or may not eventually form a complete health protocol that benefits you. This can be time-consuming, exhausting, and expensive. At Centner Wellness, we have world leading detox specialists, nutritional and immune health experts, peptide and hormonal experts, chiropractic experts, cancer and longevity experts, and so on. The collaborative efforts of our board of directors have allowed for this expertise to be available under one roof. It allows our clients to reach levels that I don't think are available anywhere else in the world.

It's also worth noting that one assessment (such as a lab) is, in many cases, only a single snapshot in time. It doesn't account for the circumstances of that moment, nor does it show what's happening throughout your system from day to day, week to week, month to month.

For example, most clinics testing for parasites only do a one-day stool test. But unless you do a three-day test (at least), you miss some of the deeper, more hidden parasites.

Finally, many assessments are based not on *healthy* levels but on *average* levels. And, news flash, the average person isn't healthy! If all a lab tells you is how you compare to unhealthy people, what good is it?

At Centner Wellness, we have comprehensive assessments, which range as deep or as basic as one requires, based on budget, beliefs, and readiness, empowering our clients to discover the root cause. Our willingness to assess more thoroughly and more deeply than anyone else comes from a desire to help those who have (a) struggled to get to the root cause of their issues and (b) continue to not have resolution or relief. Our assessment gives a full, overarching picture of the entire system, and we can work from there.

Step 2: Strengthen and Detox

The relationship between strengthening and detoxing is of critical importance for successful outcomes and proper patient safety. Your body can't effectively strengthen itself in a state of toxicity, but it also can't effectively detox unless it's strong enough. After reviewing the labs from the assessment phase, we determine whether we need to begin by first strengthening the immune system, or if our cells are strong enough, we can start with immediate detoxing.

Immune strengthening, for those who qualify, is based on cellular health. Each of our cells can have upwards of 700 mitochondria, depending on the associated organ. Our mitochondria govern our redox potential (a type of chemical reaction related to states of oxidation and our ability for our cells to regenerate). Good redox potential places your body in anti-aging, anti-disease mode.

As part of our strengthening series, we focus on cell membrane health, which requires the intake of lipids (fats) and IV PC (phosphatidylcholine, a key component of our cell membrane structure associated with accelerated regeneration and detoxification). Simultaneously, we work on strengthening the immune system. This requires testing and a specific program of micro-immunotherapy (MI) based on your individual needs. We are the only center in the United States offering micro-immunotherapy. This therapy has a long-standing history in Europe and uses low and ultra-low doses of immune system signaling molecules to bring homeostasis back to your immune system, creating balance and harmony. This is wonderful for all conditions, as they usually carry some inflammatory load and poor mitochondrial function. Together, this is a magical combinational therapy.

After the immune system is strengthened, one of the many modalities of medical detoxing we offer is chelation therapy. The word *chelation* comes from the Greek word for "claw" and refers to the process by which metal atoms "grab on" and bond to molecules such as those in your body. Over time, more and more heavy metals and toxins take hold and build up in the body, affecting how we heal and function. Chelation therapy helps shake toxins like heavy metals free from the places where they have bonded.

Many people discover that they need to detox, so they want to run quickly through the process and move on. But before we detox, we have to make sure the immune system is strong enough. Otherwise, detoxing can be more challenging than it needs to be.

There is, for example, a phenomenon known as the Herxheimer reaction, in which the process of heavy metals and toxins being rapidly pushed out and eliminated elicits a reaction from the immune system. The Herx reaction sometimes manifests as flu-like symptoms or skin conditions. If you jump right into detoxing without first opening the drainage pathways through assisted lymphatic therapy (ALT), the toxins can get stuck and cause a severe Herx reaction.

On the other hand, without detoxing, no amount of high-tech modalities or therapies you try in pursuit of strengthening will last. Even the highest volume of stem cells is compromised if you introduce them to a poisoned environment.

We run assessments before *and* after detoxing to measure the amount of heavy metals in the body. Depending on a person's toxicity load, we may need to go through two or three rounds of strengthening and detoxing. We use preservative-free IVs, vaccine-free stem cells, and only truly regenerative products that are completely toxin-free. The goal is to stop adding any products, foods, or chemicals that could continue to poison the body by putting more toxins back into the body.

For lasting results, strengthening the immune system and detoxing must go hand in hand. For this reason, we developed an immune strengthening and detoxing process that is extensive and all-encompassing, yet gentle and sustainable, providing a carefully balanced combination of these two factors for you, adjusted based on your unique health, lifestyle, and circumstances.

Step 3: Revitalize and Recharge

At Centner Wellness, we have cutting-edge medical and biohacking technology to implement treatment protocols and get results. Traditional doctors may prescribe medication to deal with health conditions, but they rarely offer suggestions to help you create a path forward. I strongly believe in the power of taking personal responsibility for your health, as opposed to living in a state of perpetual victimhood.

Let me share a quick story about one of my clients, whom we'll call Alex. He suffered from multiple forms of addiction, trauma, autoimmune conditions, and chronic pain. Alex wanted to change his health for the better, but all his experiences were a series of false starts and failures.

On the surface, it seemed like he was doing all the right things in terms of his nutrition and exercise. He confided that he'd tried every plant-based medicine under the sun and every type of therapy he could find. He would try something, have a positive experience at first, feel good for a little while, and then fall right back into his old patterns and habits.

We noticed that Alex kept using phrases like "my pain," "my addiction," "my circumstances," etc. Like many people trapped in the modern medical system, he was indoctrinated. They may have good intentions to get healthy, but over time, sicknesses, diseases, and challenges become their identities.

What Alex didn't realize was that he was severely underestimating the time required to recharge his body after these experiences. He was jumping from quick fix to quick fix without ever doing the deeper work to change his mindset or his habits, and he became increasingly discouraged each time he didn't get the results he wanted.

If you believe the problem is outside of you and that it's the doctor's responsibility to fix you, that becomes your paradigm for health. You're unconsciously making yourself a customer for life. Compare that to believing that *you* have control of your health and you can do something about it. We call this the "power transfer." This belief breakthrough work is sometimes one of the most challenging parts of the process.

Alex needed to *unlearn*. His brain was so hardwired and conditioned to be in a certain state that a large part of the process was helping him remap the neural pathways that were not serving him and empower his body to heal itself. For him, this was a prerequisite for lasting change.

Once people have woken up, they can often get back into the old ways of doing things. Even after we have changed our beliefs, let go of our past, and taken ownership, our culture still looks at driving and succeeding as the status symbol. We have to remember to pause, rest, breathe, do the things that we love, and recharge the battery of our body. We must constantly remind ourselves to rest, be still, and make our health our ultimate priority.

Fortunately, Alex brought himself from a broken place to an empowered place. He overcame multiple near-death experiences, drug addiction, and other painful and traumatic issues. With our help, he took ownership of his health and wellness, moved forward, and created a life that was in alignment with who he wanted to be. He also expanded his community and surrounded himself with people who held the same beliefs, which reflected, reinforced, and enhanced his new lifestyle. He is now inspiring other people to take their power back.

For most institutions, an individual with power over their health isn't in their best interest. They would prefer that you give your power to them. People who are healthy, well-balanced, and clear of mind don't generate as much revenue for the insurance based medical institutions. The medical institutions want *you* to empower *them* to expand and grow their business. We, on the other hand, want to help empower *you* to expand and grow *yourself*.

There's no cavalry charging in to save you. Health professionals, technologies, and tools support transformation, but if you don't change your beliefs, let go of trauma, and take full responsibility for your peace, happiness, health, and future, you're going to stay stuck in your perceived mental prison. Do you want to replay your old story, or do you want to move forward and write a new story? If you can breathe, you can still choose a path that inspires and serves you and your loved ones.

Alex's story is just one example of the importance of revitalizing and recharging to help you build a path toward the end goal: the best, healthiest, and most well-balanced version of yourself possible.

Ultimately, this process isn't just about using biohacking to heal. The entire vitality blueprint is about helping you become the proactive creator of your life, transforming you into a new, powerful being, in harmony with the journey of your destiny.

Biohacking Your Future Self: Creating a Healthier You

Picture a day when you wake up feeling energized instead of fatigued. You get out of bed full of trust in your body, eager to begin the day and excited to face any challenge it brings your way. Picture a day when your spouse, partner, or friend comes up to you and says, "Wow! I feel like I've got the old you back!" Picture a day when you can look back on your life and know that you left nothing on the table—that you used your power to make this world better, and your body served you perfectly along the way.

My goal was not only to experience all this for myself but to build a place where my team and I could bring it to the masses and create *incredible, lasting health results* that wouldn't be possible anywhere else. With Centner Wellness, I'm proud to say we have achieved just that.

I've touched on a lot of information in this short chapter. As you can imagine, no single practitioner can have *all* this knowledge. Our team of experts utilizes the expertise of world leading doctors in different areas, combining biohacking with energy healing, from regenerative medicine to plant medicine, and more, resulting in a whole-body experience that leverages the most effective modalities known to humanity and the most cutting-edge technologies on the market.

We offer bespoke healing through one of the best health assessments in the world, our 360 Assessment, which takes you through eight different tests, several high-quality consults based on your labs, and further consults after three months so we can track your progress and see how far you've come. This assessment equips you with the most personalized medical lifestyle and technology plan out there to help you overcome even the most persistent health problems. But this is only the first step. From there, we design an individualized roadmap tailored to you and only you.

One commonly asked question is, "My situation is a little bit different. Do you think you can still help me?" From experience, we can confidently tell you that the answer is yes. We've seen things you wouldn't believe, and this system has helped people from all walks of life—people just like you—heal, improve their vitality, and live their best lives.

My health journey involved exhaustive research, traveling around the world, spending lots of money, and putting myself through a great deal of trial and error to discover what worked. Fortunately, you don't have to go through all that, and you don't have to go it alone.

I encourage anyone who's curious about what we do to sign up for a complimentary "Get to Know You" consultation and tour at our world-renowned center in Brickell. Whether you've just started your healing journey, you've been at it for a few years, or you've tried every other health solution under the sun, our assessment will give you a clear path forward to the life you want.

Your journey to recovering your health doesn't have to be lonely, painful, or disjointed. With an individually tailored, comprehensive, and strategic plan, your path to vitality can be pleasant, clear, and lasting. Not only is it the right thing to do for yourself, but it's the best thing you do for your family, your business, and your legacy.

Don't put this off. The journey to biohacking your future self doesn't begin tomorrow; it begins today!

To learn more about the state-of-the-art facilities, wellness methods, biohacking technologies, and integrated medical resources available at Centner Wellness and Spa, visit centnerwellnessandspa.com, or follow us on Instagram @centnerwellness.

How can people connect with you?

You can also follow me, Leila Centner, on Instagram @leilacentner.

> **WE HAVE ALL HEARD THE SAYING "SURVIVAL OF THE FITTEST," BUT IN REALITY, IT IS SURVIVAL OF THE MOST ADAPTABLE.**
>
> *Dr. Rocco Crapis*

CHAPTER 7

MAKE YOURSELF HARDER TO KILL: BIOHACKING THE CENTRAL NERVOUS SYSTEM FOR A SOLID FOUNDATION OF HEALING BY DR. ROCCO CRAPIS

There are about six sextillion cups of water in all the oceans on planet Earth. More than *six times that many chemical reactions* occur in the human body… *per second*.

There are an estimated two trillion galaxies in the observable universe. There are up to *fifty times that many cells* in the average human body.

There are eleven systems in the body, but one of them—just one—*controls all and regulates all the others*, including *all* those cells and chemical reactions.

Many people, when they first learn about biohacking, get very excited and start shotgunning their health. They begin doing (or practicing or ingesting) every new and innovative biohack they discover. They rarely take the time to run labs first or do the appropriate foundational work to make sure they're building from a steady base.

Nevertheless, a lot of biohacks are so effective that these people likely experience some amazing results initially, even without a solid foundation. The pitfall that awaits these people is when they become dependent on supplements, therapies, and machines. Before long, they *have* to have their biohacks to feel their best—to feel normal—and if they go even a day without doing them, they start to backslide.

What we humans must realize is that as advanced as our high-tech biohacking methods are, we will never come close to being as scientifically advanced as the innate intelligence that exists within our bodies already.

"But wait," you say, "this therapy I heard about on the internet is going to change everything about my health because it initiates this incredible chemical reaction in the body to supercharge health and vitality!"

Okay, I'll see your chemical reaction and raise you a few by pointing out that 37 thousand billion billion chemical reactions occur within your body every second of your life without you ever being aware of it.

No, there was *not* a typo in that sentence: 37 *thousand billion billion* (also known as a sextillion) is 37 followed by 21 zeros. And that's the number of chemical reactions occurring within your body—not in a year, not in a day, not in a minute, but *every single second* that you draw breath.

But yes, I'm sure the one chemical reaction you're referring to is very important, too…

I realize I'm being a little flippant here, but we have to reconcile the fact that in our quest for health, the single best thing we can do is care for the system that already has all the answers, and that system, which governs every cell and tissue and organ in the body is the brain and spinal cord.

Biohacking can help you get closer to optimal vitality, but no matter how smart we think we are, our bodies are smarter. Literally, the only thing that this superintelligent system needs is to be cared for so that it can go about its business and restore life within the body as intended.

My name is Dr. Rocco Crapis. I'm a classically trained chiropractor and healer who works with adverse mechanical core tension, vibrational frequencies in the spine, emotional responses, and the upper cervical area. I serve clients across the country and around the world, and I've had firsthand experience with a ton of the biohacks you're bound to read about in this book. There is a strong focus on cellular health in the biohacking space. Unfortunately, far too few of us consider the health of the system that controls the 36 to 100 trillion cells in the average human body. Depending on the state of your system, your cells could be in a healthy, receptive, thriving state, or they could be locked in a chronic stress response.

The brain and spinal cord coordinate and control the systems of the body. And in this chapter, I'm going to show you that without a healthy central nervous system as a strong foundation for your health and wellness, all your efforts at biohacking will be no better than an ice pack on an untreated injury. It's all for nothing unless you follow an important key step *first*.

What is the "why" behind what you do?

My mission is to care for my clients by freeing up the central nervous system (CNS) so they can heal from within. In the introduction, I mentioned the eleven systems of the body. They are

1. Nervous System: Includes the central nervous system (CNS) and peripheral nervous system (PNS) and controls communication and coordination of all body functions.
2. Endocrine System: Regulates hormones through glands like the pituitary, thyroid, and adrenal glands. The CNS controls this system via the hypothalamus and pituitary gland.
3. Respiratory System: Manages breathing and gas exchange (oxygen and carbon dioxide). The brain stem regulates this through respiratory rate and rhythm.
4. Cardiovascular System: Composed of the heart and blood vessels. The CNS influences heart rate, blood pressure, and blood distribution through the autonomic nervous system.
5. Digestive System: Breaks down food, absorbs nutrients, and eliminates waste. The enteric nervous system works with the CNS to manage digestion.
6. Muscular System: Allows movement, posture, and heat production. Controlled by motor neurons from the CNS.

7. Skeletal System: Provides structure, protects organs, and supports movement. The CNS controls voluntary movements and processes sensory input from bones and joints.
8. Lymphatic System/Immune System: Defends against infection and maintains fluid balance. The CNS influences immune responses through neural and hormonal signals.
9. Urinary System: Removes waste and regulates fluid and electrolyte balance. The CNS regulates bladder function and kidney activity.
10. Reproductive System: Manages reproduction and sexual function. The CNS controls reproductive behaviors and hormonal regulation.
11. Integumentary System: Includes skin, hair, and nails, which protect the body and regulate temperature. The CNS controls sweat glands and blood flow to the skin.

Did you notice anything as I was running through that list?

The health of every organ and tissue of the body is determined by its associated system, and every system operates under the control of the central nervous system (CNS).

Everything else you need to know about human health is an expansion of this very basic but very powerful truth.

You see, there are any number of biohacks out there to address each of the systems of the body. But each of them and, by extension, the 36 to 100 trillion cells that make up the human body is controlled by your brain via the CNS.

You're probably already aware that nerves that travel down from your brain, along your spine, and out to your muscles control all your muscle contractions. It's like one big, intricate highway system inside you. And when that highway system is running smoothly, the impulses sent along those nerves from the brain can reach the intended targets and achieve the intended result. It's a perfect system by design. And it doesn't just control your muscles; it controls all those systems I just mentioned.

But what happens if that system has "roadblocks" or "construction" along the way? Those impulses become obstructed, get caught in traffic, or are forced to reroute. The signal from the nerves becomes compromised, and so does the result. The response from the organs and muscles is slower, weaker, and less efficient. Any level of strength, health, digestion, etc., can be radically enhanced with a properly functioning nervous system. And true, principled chiropractic care, quite simply, is the science of freeing up the central nervous system.

If it sounds simple, I agree. The truth usually is. But what really causes all this? What does this process look like at the biological and chemical levels?

The HPA Axis and Chronic Systemic Stress

When the body deals with a stress response, the spinal cord is the first thing to take on all that tension, and it stores those tension patterns. There's a lot I could say about this process, but we won't get into the technical stuff here. All you really need to know is that spinal tension causes the hypothalamic-pituitary-adrenal axis (HPA axis), the body's primary hormonal stress response. When this happens, the hypothalamus releases a hormone that causes a chain reaction, ultimately leading to the adrenal glands secreting cortisol. Yes, cortisol, our age-old enemy—the stress hormone responsible for helping your body respond to danger in a process sometimes referred to as the "fight-or-flight" response.

This ingenious process is meant to keep you alive during times of intense stress, uncertainty, and instability. However, when this hormonal response remains activated for a prolonged period (known by the medical term HPA axis dysfunction), the adrenal glands secrete cortisol *nonstop*. The system-wide stress response builds and builds and builds, spiraling out of control. Essentially, you've got 36–100 trillion cells in fight-or-flight mode 100% of the time.

Again, this is a defense mechanism. It's meant to keep you alive. But it's not meant to be activated for prolonged periods of time like this. Some of the symptoms of HPA axis dysfunction include high blood pressure, increased heart rate, out-of-control inflammation, decreased immune response, decreased sex hormones (yikes!), decreased dopamine... the list goes on. But arguably of even greater concern is the fact that when you are in fight-or-flight mode, your system isn't concerned with growth. Your body is just trying to survive. Everything else takes a backseat. The achievement of *optimal* health isn't a priority. Consequently, cellular DNA isn't being replicated correctly, and your cells' mitochondria can't be fed, all while the telomere is becoming shorter and shorter (this is how we identify aging).

If you've been paying attention so far, we now have

- *36 to 100 trillion cells affected by an ongoing stress response,*
- *Mitochondria that cannot be fed,*
- *Cortisol that is running rampant, and*
- *An adrenal gland being pumped dry.*

Quick note: The answer isn't an adrenal supplement. That's like putting a Band-Aid over the real problem.

Overall, the scenario listed above is the ideal breeding ground for just about every disease known to man. Even if you give your cells *perfect* input in this state, everything will still be thrown out of whack.

When it comes to biohacking, you could be doing absolutely everything right and still not be achieving the results you hoped for. It's not because you're doing something wrong. It's because you're living in a state in which your body literally cannot effectively respond!

It doesn't matter how much money you spend on therapies or supplements if you don't take care of your spine and central nervous system. I could go even deeper into the technical aspects of how this all works, but for now, suffice it to say that the prolonged, chronic stress response caused by misalignment in the spine decreases your body's adaptability over time.

Adaptability: The Key to Human Health

When there is interference between the source (the CNS) and the other ten systems of the body, it inhibits human potential. When that interference is removed and the system is unblocked, the body can release locked-up potential. Just imagine your potential if you were living with the solid foundation of a central nervous system that remains clear of interference at all times.

We have all heard the saying "survival of the fittest," but in reality, it is survival of the most adaptable. By setting yourself up with the bulletproof foundation of a clear central nervous system, every biohack you utilize for your health and wellness will be all the more effective at helping you create an organism that's more adaptable, more spiritually fulfilled, and harder to kill.

The CNS affects *everything*. I really can't stress this enough. But the system is also in a perpetual feedback loop, with your brain and spinal cord interpreting and reorganizing themselves based on what you hear, see, and do day by day, second by second. Just as we have a vast system of nerves controlling our bodies, we also have vast neural networks for everything in our lives. We form, store, and rewire this information into long-term memory that can be recalled at a moment's notice—everything from vocabulary to movement patterns. In other words, just as the CNS affects *everything* you do, *everything* you do affects the CNS.

I hope you're starting to see why it's so important to lay the right foundation. But how does this all tie into biohacking? It's very simple. Caring for the central nervous system is what makes biohacking work.

What is your favorite biohack and why?

In practice, biohacking is about enhancing human health and vitality to optimize performance and reach a level of wellness never seen before. A lot of the modalities used in the biohacking sphere are revolutionary, positively impacting human health at the cellular level.

My niche is a hyper-specific type of chiropractic care aimed at increasing human adaptability. This isn't a one-size-fits-all remedy. Increasing human adaptability looks different for everyone, but it all comes down to a fairly straightforward concept. Whatever your average is, we want to increase it to its highest level. I call it optimizing your set point. This is why **NTRS (Neural-Tension Release System)**, the type of chiropractic care I provide, is my favorite biohack. It sets the stage for literally everything else.

The P-300 wave is a measurable brainwave response associated with cognitive processing, decision-making, and attention. Often referred to as the "wave of optimal human performance," it reflects the brain's ability to process and adapt to information efficiently, making it a critical marker for well-being and human potential. By enhancing the P-300 wave through the NTRS method, we can significantly improve focus, mental clarity, and resilience. By harnessing the power of this neural response, individuals can unlock their highest levels of performance and cognitive health.

Again, if I had more space here, I could get into the intricacies of how amazing this is. We have to get the body in that receptive, balanced state so that the biohacking we're doing will be effective.

NTRS Method's Effects on Immune System Health

Does optimizing your set point mean that you'll never get sick? Not necessarily. However, when you deviate from your set point due to sickness or injury and experience symptoms, the time it takes to get back to your set point and be healthy again can be a great benchmark to judge how healthy you are.

Ideally, we want our systems to deal with anything that gets thrown our way. We want our bodies to take in any pathogen and kick its ass without us ever knowing it was even there. That said, experiencing symptomology isn't necessarily a bad thing when you're dealing with viruses, bacteria, and toxins. Being at your optimal level of health means that your body's response will be more effective.

The mistake that many people (and many doctors) make is to treat the symptoms, not the cause. When you step on a dog's tail, it barks. Treating symptoms instead of treating the underlying cause is like trying to silence the bark while there's still a boot on the poor dog's tail.

A fever is a great example. Just like the HPA axis response mentioned earlier, a fever is a defense mechanism. Most viruses cannot live at high temperatures, so when a virus gets in, your body kicks up its internal temperature to quite literally bake the invader to death. It's a normal physiological response. Unfortunately, a fever isn't always comfortable. If we take a fever reducer to ease that discomfort, it lowers the body's temperature. This can cause the virus to get a stronger hold, replicate, and persist much longer within the body. Of course, you have to monitor this—there are times when fevers can reach dangerous levels and must be lowered, but there is a threshold we're supposed to live at.

Why is it that some people who are exposed to COVID-19 are down for a day/week, while for others, it's more like a month? Why are some people still fighting symptoms *a year later*, and why do some people never recover at all? And what about the ones who get exposed to COVID-19 and are only sick for a day or two or never experience *any* symptoms? Are they just lucky? Why such a wide range of responses?

The difference is adaptability and the body's ability to respond effectively. And it all starts with having a clear spine and central nervous system. This must be firmly established before you try to build on it with biohacking.

Remember those 36 to 100 trillion cells I mentioned earlier? Well, your body is constantly recycling them, giving birth to new ones as the old ones die. Inside of you, an estimated 330 billion new cells are created every day. If you do the math, that means that technically, every 87 days, you're a new person.

If you're living with tension on the spinal cord and interference in the CNS, the 330 billion cells created today are less than thriving specimens. Thus, by extension, the new person you become in 87 days will be a less than thriving specimen, too. The new you will be in a state of dis-ease (the opposite of ease).

By contrast, as soon as you're adjusted and your central nervous system is clear, your body instantly starts making 330 billion new *correct* cells, increasing your adaptability and exponentially enhancing the expression of health in your body. The very instant your central nervous system is clear, the cells that are created have a new vibration.

Yes, we can use biohacking methods to create amazing results. But if your spinal cord is in misalignment and is choking your central nervous system, it's like you're swimming against the current—fighting against your body.

In 87 days, you will surely be an entirely new you, one way or another.

May Your House Stand Firm

In the Parable of the Wise and Foolish Builders, Jesus Christ taught that the foolish man built his house on the sand, but the wise man built his house on the rock. When the rains came, the foolish man's house was washed away, but the wise man's house stood firm.

So, where are you building your proverbial house? Have you wisely laid down a strong foundation for your health, or will it be washed away with the first flood?

Biohacking isn't meant to be the new pharmaceutical crutch. We're all striving to reach the next level. Just make sure you're stepping up to that level from a solid foundation. And in your search for the latest and greatest biohack to help you thrive, do not neglect the most ancient and most powerful factor of human health: caring for the brain, the spinal cord, and the central nervous system.

NTRS is different. It's focused on how the entire system functions as one continuous, interdependent organ, as opposed to treating it as segmented pieces. You're not going to find this level of care anywhere else. Believe me, I have clients who have looked, and it's why they continue to seek me out from around the world. Come visit me to try out NTRS and see how your world changes as you biohack your way toward all-terrain adaptability to become an organism that's harder to kill!

How can people connect with you?

I can be found at alchemychiro.com and on Instagram @thedr.rocco.

HUMAN BEINGS ARE WIRED FOR CONNECTION. IT IS ESSENTIAL FOR OUR SURVIVAL, BOTH PHYSICALLY AND EMOTIONALLY.

Eileen Lemelman

CHAPTER 8

THE HEALING POWER OF CONNECTION: A BIOHACK FOR MENTAL HEALTH BY EILEEN LEMELMAN

How can someone grow up in a house full of people and still feel entirely alone?
I did.

I grew up in a big family—five children, to be exact—but loneliness was my constant companion. Maybe it was because I was the only girl with four brothers, longing for the sister I'd never have. Or maybe it was the secrets I learned to keep because of my alcoholic father. Perhaps it was being Jewish in a world that seemed to revolve around Christmas trees and Sunday Church services.

Whatever the reason, I often felt like I didn't belong. Like I was on the outside, looking in—a silent observer of a life I didn't feel invited to live. It was as if my family was the cast of a movie from the edges, waiting for a role that never came.

Those early experiences of loneliness shaped me in profound ways. Loneliness has a strange irony; it can either isolate you further or propel you to seek deeper connections. For me, it was the latter.

It might seem counterintuitive, but some of us who know the ache of loneliness choose careers where the connection is central—like becoming a therapist. For those of us who have felt invisible, unheard, or on the outside, helping others find belonging can become a calling. That was my experience. The loneliness I carried and the sense of never truly belonging shaped me into someone who was deeply empathetic, someone who could sit with others in their pain and offer them the connection I so desperately craved. It became not just a career but a mission—a way to turn my struggles into a source of healing for others.

And over time, that deep sense of being an outsider transformed into something more—it became my purpose, my "why." Those early experiences of loneliness ignited a passion within me to create spaces where women could come together, feel seen, heard, and truly connected. I wanted to build what I had longed for: a community where women no longer felt on the outside, but firmly embraced within.

These early experiences of loneliness shaped me in profound ways. They made me deeply empathetic to others who feel like they do not belong and who navigate life with a sense of disconnection. Over time, that sense of being an outsider inspired my life's work—creating spaces where women could come together, feel seen, and connect on a deeper level. This mission became especially clear after the pandemic.

It wasn't until the COVID-19 pandemic, when loneliness and isolation reached unprecedented levels, that the true scope of the problem became impossible to ignore. Researchers had long identified loneliness as a growing concern, but lockdowns forced the world to recognize the symptoms of loneliness as "epidemic." And women—especially midlife women—were among the hardest hit.

Midlife women often face life transitions that quietly steal their sense of connection and belonging. Empty nests, the loss of a spouse through death or divorce, relocations, career shifts, and retirement all chip away at their social fabric. Many women report feeling irrelevant, sexually unattractive, and invisible, as though they no longer matter. The isolation of the pandemic only magnified these struggles.

During this time, I witnessed firsthand how deeply women were struggling—not just with anxiety, depression, and uncertainty of the pandemic, but with a much deeper loneliness. It wasn't about being physically alone; it was the emotional and social isolation that weighed most heavily.

And with that realization came a responsibility I couldn't ignore. I had a calling—to step forward, not just for one woman at a time but for all midlife women navigating the emotional, mental, physical, and social challenges that so often leave them feeling alone. These women deserved a voice, someone to stand with them, and remind them they didn't have to bear these challenges in silence or isolation; this was my mission.

The COVID-19 pandemic altered how we live and connect. Social distancing, lockdowns, and prolonged isolation disrupted our routines and severed the small, everyday moments of connection that sustain us—hugs, handshakes, shared meals, and even casual conversations. These acts of touch and togetherness release oxytocin, the feel-good hormone that strengthens bonds and fosters a sense of well-being. Without them, loneliness deepened, leaving many people struggling with emotional and social isolation. Research confirmed what many of us felt: levels of loneliness surged during the pandemic, highlighting the damaging consequences of prolonged isolation on mental health.

Faced with this epidemic of disconnection, the importance of community became undeniable. Community is more than just a network of people; it is a lifeline. It reduces the negative effects of stress, fosters resilience, and provides the social support we need to navigate life's challenges. Belonging to a community can cultivate hope and optimism—powerful antidotes to loneliness—by reminding us that we are not alone in our struggles. In community, we find people who see us, listen to us, and stand with us, allowing us to heal together. In these shared spaces of belonging, we rediscover our strength, reconnect with others, and build the resilience needed to weather life's storms.

During this time of immense isolation, I was working one-on-one with clients via Zoom. Week after week, I saw women struggling, not only with the anxiety and uncertainty of the pandemic but also with a deeper sense of loneliness. And I realized I had a bigger responsibility—a calling. I could not just focus on helping individual women in my practice. I needed to be the voice for midlife women facing these challenges. Women navigating the physical, emotional, and spiritual changes of their lives often feel alone. This realization propelled me to create spaces for connection. I declared, "We need each other. We cannot, nor should we, do this alone." It is never too late to make changes in our lives to feel empowered, and I knew that belonging to a community—a tribe of women—was the solution.

With this calling in mind, I made a shift. I worked as a licensed clinical social worker in private practice for years, helping individuals overcome personal challenges and mental health concerns. But moving from a one-to-one model to a one-to-many model came with a set of challenges. Building an audience took time, patience, and an unwavering commitment. Even though I knew so many women were struggling with loneliness, finding ways to connect them in meaningful ways was not always straightforward.

I learned many lessons as I transitioned into entrepreneurship, using my clinical skills to reach and support more women. First, it became clear that the need for connection was even more significant than I imagined. Women were desperate for a place to be seen, heard, and validated. However, gathering this audience required trust, consistency, and a safe, nurturing environment where the women felt comfortable opening up.

Although the research shows that most women have at least one close friend, the discrepancy lies in the quality of that relationship versus the relationship they would like to have. Many women confide in me that while they have friends, these relationships often lack depth. They long for connections that go beyond surface-level conversations. This desire for deeper, more meaningful relationships is where many women feel stuck.

Loneliness often carries with it a sense of shame and failure. Many women feel compelled to hide their loneliness, as though admitting they are searching for a connection makes them weak or unworthy. However, I have learned that sharing these struggles within a supportive community can transform these feelings of shame into empowerment. This inspired the SistHER group, which I founded to create a safe space for women to gather and connect authentically.

In our SistHER group, we gather monthly, often theming our meetings around seasons and holidays, using these as touchstones to explore issues relevant to midlife women. Each meeting offers an opportunity for social connection, a powerful avenue for healing.

One of the most transformative gatherings centered on forgiveness, a topic we chose to coincide with the Jewish Day of Atonement—a time dedicated to reflection, repentance, and seeking forgiveness.

We began, as always, with a meditation to cultivate peace and openness. Then, we engaged in a symbolic exercise: writing down our deepest hurts and emotions on paper and ceremonially burning them—a ritual of release and surrender. The impact was profound. Many SistHERS shared that they could finally forgive their fathers, mothers, or siblings for long-held wounds. Letting go not only facilitated personal healing, but also deepened our connections with one another.

The emotional benefits of such deep relationships are immense. Feeling understood, supported, and valued creates a safe space for vulnerability. It fosters a sense of belonging, enhances happiness, and boosts self-esteem. Sharing intimate thoughts and emotions with those who genuinely listen cultivates strong bonds and intimacy.

Building and nurturing these relationships is a vital biohack for well-being. The sense of belonging and community we cultivate in SistHER is not just comforting; it's essential! It empowers us to face life's challenges with resilience and optimism, reminding us that we are never truly alone.

Our SistHER group has become a sanctuary where women feel empowered to share their deepest fears, worries, and anxieties, knowing they are not alone. One SistHER expressed, "Despite my ongoing fears, I realize that every month I manage to reach my personal finish line with the help and support of my SistHERS." Others have echoed similar sentiments, finding inner strength and peace through our collective support.

This transformation—from isolation and negative mindsets to a sense of belonging and connection brimming with possibility—is profound. With the group's support, members are learning to reframe their fears and anxieties into helpful outcomes. This communal reinforcement embodies a powerful biohack: leveraging deep, supportive relationships to enhance mental and emotional well-being. By embracing the strength of community, we realize that we don't have to navigate life's challenges alone; together, we cultivate resilience, optimism, and a renewed sense of purpose.

Meaningful relationships within our SistHER group profoundly impact both emotional and physical well-being. Engaging in supportive social interactions stimulates the release of neurotransmitters like dopamine, oxytocin, and serotonin, often referred to as "happy hormones." These chemicals play distinct roles in enhancing mood and health.

The emotional effects of these neurotransmitters include feelings of pleasure, happiness, contentment, trust, bonding, and a sense of well-being. Physically, they contribute to reduced stress, improved immune function, and increased physical intimacy. These hormones promote positive social connections and contribute to overall health and happiness.

As the group grows, I am continually amazed by the true intimate connections formed between the women. These bonds are deep, genuine, and healing—proof that it is possible to find meaningful relationships when we step into a community with open hearts and vulnerability.

What is the "why" behind what I do?

The "why" behind my work is deeply personal and rooted in the loneliness and isolation that so many of us faced during and after the COVID-19 pandemic. During this time, I witnessed firsthand how disconnection from the world affected me and countless women in midlife who were already navigating challenging life transitions. This experience solidified my mission: creating spaces where women can come together, rediscover their purpose, and feel truly seen and connected.

The reality is stark: the number of people who live alone has increased by over 30% in the last few decades. Social isolation is considered as harmful to our health as smoking fifteen cigarettes a day, and loneliness can increase the risk of premature death by up to 50%. The latest research echoes findings from the *Campaign to End Loneliness*, which revealed that women are more likely than men to experience chronic loneliness.

Many factors contribute to this epidemic of loneliness, particularly among midlife women. Widowhood often leaves older women living alone, and hormone changes from menopause can lead to depression, exacerbating feelings of disconnection. There is also the phenomenon of "Invisible Woman Syndrome," where women feel increasingly overlooked in social situations, the workplace, and media representation. Health changes, such as hearing and vision loss, memory issues, and disability can also isolate women further, especially when coupled with the loss of friends, distance from their family, retirement, and shrinking social networks.

The effects of loneliness and social isolation are profound. On a mental level, loneliness can lead to anxiety, depression, emotional distress, and even suicidal thoughts. It can contribute to cognitive decline and dementia. Physically, the risks are alarming—loneliness can increase the likelihood of high blood pressure, heart disease, stroke, type 2 diabetes, and obesity. Loneliness also weakens the immune system, making it harder for the body to fight off illness. On a behavioral level, lonely individuals may be more likely to smoke, overuse alcohol, and struggle with sleep. They may also choose to engage in healthy activities like exercise.

Loneliness affects brain health, making everyday tasks such as cooking or paying bills more difficult. It also increases inflammation in the body, leading to fatigue, inactivity, and a depressed mood.

These issues became more visible during the pandemic, which heightened the loneliness epidemic and amplified the mental and physical health risks associated with isolation. I saw the deep need for connection, not only for survival but for women to thrive. This is why I created the SistHER group, a community where women could come together, share their stories, and find strength in each other. I have seen how true, intimate connections can change lives, and my mission is to create spaces where these bonds can flourish.

How have you pivoted your business in the last few years?

For years as a psychotherapist and licensed clinical social worker, I operated within a very structured, rigid framework—one that insurance companies and the state monitored. There was comfort in that structure. It gave me clear guidelines to follow, and for a long time, I did not question it. But after the pandemic, something inside me shifted. I realized the comfortable box I had been working in was no longer enough. It was safe but not fulfilling the deeper calling that had been stirring within me.

The pandemic amplified feelings of loneliness and anxiety for many women, and I felt that I could not stay within the old confines. There was something more I needed to offer. I had a calling to help women who were not just battling mental health challenges but who were feeling profoundly alone, unseen, and unsupported. I was not just meant to sit within the boundaries of the clinical world; I was called to be a light and a voice for these women. I wanted to celebrate their resilience and their successes in overcoming adversity, but I also knew something else was needed—education. To truly destigmatize the need for help and encourage women to reach out for support, I had to think differently.

One of the most significant shifts I made was incorporating the power of community into my work. There is something transformative about women coming together, especially in a group setting. Meditation in community is especially powerful. The collective energy created in a shared space brings a sense of calm and connection that cannot be replicated alone. A positive environment emerges when women gather in a safe, nurturing, and supportive place.

In this setting, women can let their walls down. They realize that they do not have to carry their burdens alone, allowing them to open up in ways they never could before.

But this realization did not come without its challenges. For years, I operated in a space where my vulnerability was not encouraged. I was trained to keep my story separate, to maintain a distance. But as I started to work with these women, I realized that to connect truly, I had to step out from behind that professional wall. It was a moment of reckoning for me because vulnerability felt so unfamiliar in my role as a therapist. Yet, I knew deep down that I had to be authentic to reach the women who were suffering.

The hardest part was allowing myself to share my story—to show my struggles and let them see that I was not just a clinician but a woman who understood pain and loneliness too. I knew it was not standard in the clinical world, but I realized my story could help destigmatize the need for support. By being open and vulnerable, I could create the connection that these women needed to feel safe enough to seek help.

It was not an easy transition, but it was necessary. In that process, I have found that the women I work with can connect more deeply—not only with me but with each other—and that is where the real healing begins.

What is your favorite biohack and why?

My favorite biohack, without a doubt, is connecting in community. I have struggled with low-level depression throughout my life, and I have learned that one of the most profound ways to lift myself out of those dark moments is through human connection. When I am feeling low, it is easy to isolate myself, but I have come to understand that the very act of engaging with others—of being part of a community—can change everything. It is like a lifeline. The moment I interact, share, and feel heard, that sense of being alone fades, and my mood shifts.

What is biohacking? It is the art and science of taking control of your biology, and manipulating the environment inside and outside of yourself so you can program it to perform at any level you want and supercharge the results. For me, community is one of the most powerful biohacks because it does not just lift us emotionally; it supercharges the impact of healing. When you connect with others, especially in a tribe of like-minded people, you are not only programming your brain and body for better health, but you are amplifying the effects through collective support.

Human beings are wired for connection. It is essential for our survival, both physically and emotionally. We thrive in community because that is how we are designed to function—we lean on each other, learn from each other, and find strength in shared experiences. For women, this is especially important. Women need women. Throughout history, we have come together in groups to nurture, support, and lift each other up. There is something incredibly powerful about being in a space where you are understood and valued by others who have faced similar challenges.

Belonging to a community and feeling a sense of belonging is essential to healing. It is more than being around people—it is about genuinely feeling seen, heard, and valued. Feeling like we belong helps regulate our nervous system, calming the body's stress response and allowing us to feel safe and grounded. That sense of belonging allows us to heal and grow.

During the pandemic, I felt that need for others more than ever, and I observed so many of my patients suffering in isolation. Loneliness affects our mental health profoundly, increasing depression, anxiety, and even addiction. Substance abuse, gambling, online shopping, overeating, and suicides surged during this time. It creates a painful cycle—loneliness leads to depression, which leads to further withdrawal, and the cycle repeats. But when we connect in a community, we break that cycle. We create a safe space to support each other and heal together.

The isolation brought on by the COVID-19 pandemic underscored the need for connection, prompting me to adopt a hybrid approach for the SistHER group. We expanded our community beyond local boundaries by offering in-person and virtual options, embracing members from various locations. This inclusivity ensures no one feels alone; community is always accessible, regardless of physical distance.

Born from the isolation of the pandemic and the longing for connection, the SistHER group addresses the profound effect of loneliness on our emotional and physical health. Through this hybrid model, we unlock women's ultimate potential by fostering meaningful connections, supporting each other through life's challenges, and proving that we do not have to face anything alone. Precisely the impetus for writing my book "Circle of Sisterhood: Lonely No More. Together, we thrive.

How can people connect with you?

I can be found at www.eileenlemelman.com and you can connect with me at eileen.lemelman@gmail.com

UNLEASH YOUR INNER WARRIOR AND EMBRACE THE JOURNEY OF BEING UNAPOLOGETICALLY YOU. LIVE WITH HEARTFELT AUTHENTICITY, ACT WITH COURAGE, AND ALWAYS PRIORITIZE YOUR WELL-BEING.

Sandra Salce

CHAPTER 9

MY STORY: A JOURNEY TO OWNING WELLNESS BY SANDRA SALCE

My Journey to Entrepreneurship

Growing up, I held onto a dream as bright as the stars—to become an Olympic gymnast. The glittering vision of competing on the world stage was my guiding light, and I was willing to make any sacrifice for it. Missing friends' birthday parties, school events, and even family gatherings didn't phase me because I was doing what I loved. Every moment spent in the gym, every hour dedicated to perfecting my routines, filled me with an incomparable sense of purpose and joy. The thrill of landing a flawless routine or mastering a new skill was unmatched by anything else in my life.

Those sacrifices, which might have seemed enormous to others, were stepping stones on the path to my dreams. The camaraderie with my teammates, the unwavering support of my coaches, and the exhilarating rush of competitions made every challenge worthwhile.

However, at fifteen, my journey took an unexpected turn. A misdiagnosed Achilles tear shattered my dream, forcing me to confront a harsh new reality and pushing me in an entirely different direction. What initially felt like a devastating setback turned out to be life's way of gently steering me toward a future brimming with wondrous adventures and opportunities that I never could have imagined. This unexpected twist in my path proved that sometimes the most remarkable experiences stem from the most unforeseen changes.

By eighteen, I had pivoted to the travel industry, driven by aspirations of exploring the globe and becoming a high-powered professional. My enthusiasm for discovery and adventure propelled me forward, and at twenty, I married and set out to conquer the challenges of adulthood. Yet, by twenty-three, I found myself navigating the tumultuous waters of a newly divorced single mom. It was in these moments of vulnerability and uncertainty that I learned one of life's most profound lessons: life doesn't always go as envisioned, and it does not come with a manual.

Each twist and turn, each high and low, taught me to embrace the unpredictability of life. It was through these experiences that I understood the importance of putting my best foot forward and making the most of every single moment. The resilience I cultivated during these years would become a cornerstone of my entrepreneurial journey.

Through these experiences, I learned several things about myself:

- I discovered my inner strength and resilience. No matter what life threw at me, I learned I had the power to overcome it. This realization not only gave me confidence but also prepared me for future challenges.
- I uncovered my warrior spirit, which drove me forward and kept me motivated, even in the face of adversity.
- I realized that my survival instincts were not just confined to the gym but extended to all aspects of life. This understanding highlighted my ability to adapt and thrive in any situation.

These lessons would later define my entrepreneurial journey, shaping me into a resilient, determined, and adaptable individual. I came to understand that life could not break me, and no matter what challenges I faced, I could overcome them. This unwavering belief in my ability to prevail became the bedrock of my personal and professional growth.

Innovation and creativity marked the early years of my childhood. I was always coming up with ideas for new tools and gadgets. However, these ambitious projects often fizzled out due to a lack of feasibility and resources. The absence of a college degree weighed heavily on me, deepening my sense of inadequacy. These doubts and insecurities created a barrier to my aspirations, holding me back from reaching higher goals.

Additionally, having an absentee father whom I was very close to, and who deceived me, left me feeling profoundly unwanted. His absence in my life created a void that no amount of innovation or creativity could fill. I yearned for his presence, his guidance, and his love, but all I was met with was silence and broken promises. At the age of twelve, he shattered the bond we shared when he walked away to create a new family and never looked back. I was left questioning my worth and place in the world, wondering how I could be so easily replaced.

This feeling of abandonment cast a long shadow over my formative years. Each unfulfilled promise and missed milestone chipped away at my sense of self-worth. I often felt like an outcast, struggling to navigate life without the support of someone who was supposed to be my pillar of strength. The betrayal I felt was a heavy burden to carry, and it colored every aspect of my life.

Despite my creative spark, the pain of feeling unwanted and deceived by someone so close to me made it difficult to believe in myself and my dreams. My aspirations seemed like distant stars, beautiful but out of reach. The emotional scars left by my father's absence were deep, and they took years to heal. Yet, in those darkest moments, I found the strength to push forward and redefine my path.

Over time, through deep introspection, I realized that my inner strength became my guiding light. Amidst these moments of reflection, I unearthed a pivotal truth: the only obstacle truly holding me back was myself. My insecurities had been the chains that shackled me, keeping me from realizing my limitless potential. As I began to accept and embrace my unique capabilities, I came to a profound understanding that my worth was not defined by a mere degree or love from a father I once knew, but by the unyielding determination, perseverance, and inner fortitude that I possessed. It was this relentless inner drive to effect change that sparked a profound transformation within me, enabling me to break free from the self-imposed limitations that had previously confined my path.

My journey has been defined by an undeniable resilience and a spirit that refuses to be subdued. Born at just twenty-six weeks, weighing a fragile 2 lbs. 4 oz and measuring a mere 14 inches, I entered this world against overwhelming odds. The doctors didn't expect me to survive; they warned my parents to prepare for the worst. Even though I hadn't realized it then, my fighting spirit shone from the very beginning. I spent the first three months of my life in an incubator, a tiny warrior battling for every breath. My eyelids were still fused together, and my lungs hadn't fully developed yet. The medical staff often marveled at my constant movement, as I wiggled out of my swaddle with such determination that they had to tie me down to keep me safe. It was evident, even then, that my fight was not just about survival; it was a relentless pursuit of a life fully lived. I was too young to comprehend it, but that indomitable spirit set the tone for my entire life. That same fervor propelled me through countless highs and lows, with each obstacle only fortifying my inner warrior. Every challenge I faced reinforced the unyielding spirit that has defined my existence, transforming every setback into a stepping stone for greater achievements.

In my early fifties, I faced one of the most significant trials of my life. Constant pain left me unable to rise from my bed without rolling to my side. This daily struggle illuminated a crucial truth: my perspective on fitness needed a fundamental shift. I have been dedicated to fitness since the age of ten, experimenting with all kinds of workouts—from sports to weightlifting, CrossFit, low-impact, and everything in between. I explored every avenue in pursuit of physical excellence, often competing with people half my age. Whether I slept a full eight hours or just two, skipping a workout was never an option. From my days of training in gymnastics six hours a day, six days a week, with weekends filled with competitions, health, wellness, and fitness was ingrained in my DNA.

Despite my dedication, the wear and tear from overworking my body took its toll, intensifying the pain in my muscles and joints. It became clear that my approach needed to evolve. This realization led me to a pursuit of finding a fitness regimen that I could do at any age and at any level. I understood that my drive had to be balanced with a more sustainable and holistic approach to health, wellness, and fitness, one that would allow me to continue my journey without compromising my body. It was then that I understood that I couldn't continue pushing myself to the breaking point, enduring days, weeks, even months to recovery. The debilitating pain was a harsh revelation—if life is marked by pain, movement ceases, and with that stillness, aging accelerates. As someone who had always excelled and thrived on achievement, the emotional turmoil left me feeling lost and deeply frustrated, questioning my ability to continue performing at my best.

In addition, when my youngest daughter left for college, the transition to an empty nest brought a significant shift in my life. Having first become a mom at twenty-three and then again at thirty-six, I was used to focusing my energy on my children. Not having someone to concentrate on and now directing all my time toward myself was an enormous challenge to overcome. The once vibrant and bustling home now echoed with silence, offering me a chance for deep introspection. It was in these quiet moments that I realized a significant truth: despite the many changes I had experienced, my purpose had always been constant. The drive to nurture and help others live their healthiest, best lives was deeply ingrained in me, extending far beyond the role of a mother. As I adjusted to this new chapter, I recognized the need to concentrate on nurturing and taking care of my health while inspiring others. This realization, coupled with a desire to make a meaningful impact, motivated me to explore new opportunities.

After dedicating thirty-eight years to the corporate world, and with the encouragement of my supportive husband and remarkable daughters, I took a bold leap of faith and opened my HOTWORX franchise— HOTWORX Deerfield Beach! Running my studio feels like nurturing an extended family. We extend a warm welcome and encouragement to every member who walks through our doors. I believe in creating a supportive, inclusive environment where everyone feels valued and motivated to achieve their best. We celebrate each other's milestones, big or small, and support one another through challenges. This sense of belonging and camaraderie is the heart of our studio, because it's *my* heart. It's not just about the workouts; it's about building relationships and fostering a space where people can feel seen, wanted, and at home.

Opening a HOTWORX franchise was more than a business venture—it was the fulfillment of my lifelong purpose. Throughout my life, I had always instilled the importance of fitness into my children, encouraging them to lead active and healthy lifestyles. This new chapter allowed me to integrate my passion for health, wellness, and fitness with my newfound focus on self-care. This revelation reinforced my commitment to promoting a healthier life, not only for myself but for others as well. It was a reminder that my identity as a nurturer and caregiver was an integral part of who I am, and that by taking care of myself, I could better empower others to live their healthiest, most vibrant lives.

Though the path was challenging, my unwavering passion, combined with the transformative benefits of infrared energy, heat, and exercise, became life-changing. Though I cannot reverse the aging process, healing through heat and movement was the key to a pain-free life. This shift allowed me to rediscover the joy of movement and reclaim my vitality. Working out smarter, not harder—from the inside out—transformed my approach to health, wellness, and fitness, becoming my mantra.

Through this journey, I learned to embrace acceptance within myself. The doubts I once harbored, reminiscent of my early years, gradually dissipated. This venture transcended the realm of business; it became the manifestation of a lifelong dream and the dawn of a transformative chapter in my life. It turns out that what I once perceived as failures were merely stepping stones in my life's story. Each one served as a powerful reminder that I have always been a fighter. Despite my deep-rooted insecurities, this journey opened my eyes to the boundless potential within me. Embracing this truth allowed me to understand that becoming a business owner was not just a professional triumph; it was a deeply personal one. Many of us go through life believing that money or success determines our worth, but in reality, it's defined by how we rise after we fall. My becoming an entrepreneur symbolized my growth and resilience, reinforcing that I can overcome any obstacle and realize my dreams.

My life has been marked by countless obstacles and trials, but as I often remind my daughters, "Good things take effort, but anything from the heart is well worth it." Through these challenges, I understand that true success isn't measured by monetary profit alone, but by the fulfillment of genuine needs. When a business meets a real need, the financial rewards naturally follow, and the impact on people's lives becomes the most meaningful measure of success.

From overcoming self-doubt to navigating the complexities of starting a business, each obstacle taught me valuable lessons. I learned the importance of resilience, adaptability, perseverance, and the importance of staying laser-focused on the bigger picture. In business, like in life, things don't always go as you envisioned, but in the end, it all works out. Every doubt, obstacle, and challenge is not a failure but an opportunity to learn and grow. One of the most significant lessons I learned was the importance of mentorship and support. Seeking guidance from experienced entrepreneurs helped me avoid common pitfalls and helped me make informed decisions.

My ultimate destination on this incredible journey as a franchisee has been the creation of a vibrant and nurturing health and wellness community through HOTWORX. I have built a sanctuary, where like-minded individuals can come together to enhance not only their physical well-being but also their mental and emotional well-being. The joy and fulfillment I experience when I see members discovering their *inner warrior* by reaching their health milestones, overcoming pain, and reclaiming their lives is beyond measure. Each success story reaffirms my belief in the transformative power of dedication, support, movement, and the healing benefits of infrared therapy.

From the spark of a childhood dream to the resilient spirit in the face of life's adversities, this journey is a testament to triumph over obstacles. It is a profound and transformative experience that underscores the essential importance of physical recovery and the cultivation of smart, sustainable health habits. This odyssey not only showcases the indomitable human spirit but also highlights the incredible power of perseverance, healing, and holistic well-being. Unleash your *inner warrior* and embrace the journey of being unapologetically you. Live with heartfelt authenticity, act with courage, and always prioritize your well-being. Be You! Do You! For You! This is your unique story—embrace it fully and make it your own.

What is the "why" behind what you do?

My *why* is deeply rooted in my passion for living life to the fullest and helping others achieve a healthier lifestyle. I am driven by a desire to feel my best and help others do the same because I learned early on that my *why* is not based on how others see my worth but on how I see it. The benefits of infrared energy, heat, and exercise have helped me heal both emotionally and physically, and I want to inspire and help others to live pain-free and vibrant lives. This passion is fueled by my experiences, and I believe that health and wellness are essential for a fulfilling life.

What unique framework or service do you offer to your community or clients?

At HOTWORX, we offer a unique workout experience that promotes recovery, reduces pain, and improves overall well-being. HOTWORX uses far infrared radiation (FIR), sometimes referred to as thermal radiation. FIR has the ability to penetrate the skin and underlying tissues up to 1.5 inches from the surface of the skin. When FIR radiation penetrates human cells, it generates heat, but it also changes the molecular vibrations. In other words, the waves of FIR cause new vibrations at the cellular level. These new "vibes" are beneficial to your health. Studies show that the use of infrared saunas assists in weight loss, reduction of muscle soreness, helps with pain management, skin purification, detoxification, stress reduction, anti-aging, and much more.

Our infrared sauna heats the body and penetrates deeply into joints, muscles, and tissues, speeding oxygen flow and increasing circulation. The increase in core body temperature and circulation will burn more calories at a faster rate than what you would find with a traditional workout. Our approach emphasizes working out smarter, not harder, to achieve optimal health. This innovative approach to fitness allows our members to experience the benefits of infrared energy, leading to improved physical and mental health.

How have you pivoted your business in the last few years?

We've adapted to the changing landscape by incorporating virtually instructed sessions designed for busy lifestyles with 24/7 access and 15–30-minute workouts. This flexibility has allowed us to continue supporting our members' health and wellness goals, even during challenging times.

How were you able to transform a setback into a setup for success?

My Achilles tear, which once seemed like a career-ending injury, ultimately led me to discover my true calling in health and wellness. This setback became the foundation for my success as an entrepreneur. It taught me the importance of resilience and adaptability, and it reinforced my belief that every challenge is an opportunity for growth.

What role do collaboration and community have in your business?

Collaboration and community are at the heart of HOTWORX. We foster a supportive environment and a sense of belonging because together we can reach our goals and achieve more. This strong sense of community has been instrumental in building a thriving and successful business.

What advice would you give to someone considering entrepreneurship?

Believe in yourself and your vision, even when faced with doubts. Seek mentorship, plan meticulously, and remember that success comes in various forms. Stay resilient and adapt to challenges along the way. Your passion and determination will guide you through the ups and downs of entrepreneurship.

What is your favorite biohack and why?

My favorite biohack is incorporating HOTWORX's Infrared Energy, Heat and Exercise for More Workout In Less Time! Its virtual instructed 15–30-minute workouts, 24/7 access and affordability allows me to incorporate this into my daily life. Its 3-D training method enhances recovery, reduces pain, and promotes overall well-being, allowing me to maintain an active, healthier lifestyle as I age. This innovative approach to fitness has been a game-changer for me, and I am passionate about sharing its benefits with others. I just wish I had found HOTWORX sooner.

How can people connect with you?

I can be found on my website at: www.hotworx.net/studio/deerfieldbeach-shoppesatdeerfield and on Instagram and Facebook @HOTWORXDeerfieldBeach.

WHEN YOU KNOW HOW TO READ YOUR INTUITION, IT'S LIKE LEARNING A NEW LANGUAGE. IT OPENS UP A WHOLE NEW WORLD OF OPPORTUNITIES.

Jawna Standish

CHAPTER 10

WHAT DOES YOUR GUT INSTINCT SAY?
BY JAWNA STANDISH

> *"A Longevity Mindset means becoming the 'CEO of your own health' and recognizing that 'Life is short, until you extend it.'"*
> —Peter Diamandis, M.D. & Futurist

It was the searing heat, bright sunshine, and waves that woke me up. That's how it all began. My calling found me. Actually, I think we were always destined to meet. It was only a matter of time.

Before work, I would put on my bathing suit, head to the cockpit, look toward the sun and give thanks to the Universe for the sea I was about to dive into. This nourished me, like some sort of religious ritual. Every day. So there I was, living and working as a digital nomad on our sailboat having Google Meet calls with clients.

I was completely unaware of any underwater disturbances happening beneath me. The waves were about to travel in all directions from the point of disturbance with such immense speed and force, I wouldn't even see it coming. I never thought I could survive something of that magnitude. Yet here I am.

The Tsunami

My journey into biohacking, neuroscience, and longevity science didn't begin with a mystical experience, a venture-backed start-up, or a childhood dream of becoming a doctor. In fact, I chose to keep it like this: The person I trusted the most betrayed me, and I was left displaced in ways I'd never imagined.

Everything I thought was my reality was now distorted. Gravity felt like it no longer existed. This betrayal impacted my mind, body, health, business, relationships, and life.

I *chose* not to be a victim.

I *chose* love and empowerment.

I *chose* to serve; otherwise I knew I would always be a prisoner.

My biohacking mission or message is about transforming and thriving. It's about understanding that the greatest superpower and longevity secret you have as a human is not in a pill, an injection, or on the next trip to Mars. As a scientist, I will tell you this: It's something you already possess inside of you. You might not know it yet. I'm going to tell you.

My biohack is understanding the science and secret wisdom of your intuition so you can leverage it to elevate your reach and impact in your business, health, and relationships. Your intuition is the most underrated tool you have in your life. Are you using it to its fullest capacity? To your advantage? I bet you never thought of that. Most of us don't, so don't worry.

Most of us take our intuition for granted or are unaware that it's our greatest tool in life. It's what's kept us on this earth for so long, in fact. Yet, research and expert insights suggest that many people are unaware of how to recognize, trust, and apply their intuition consciously for optimized business, health, and relationships.

This is what I have focused my research and work on: the science and secret wisdom of intuition.

Sometimes all you need is a sign from the Universe that you're in the right place to discover something new about yourself. If you were ever looking for that sign, let this be the one.

Living the Digital Nomad Life

From the outside, my life looked like some Instagram travel blogger life, moonlighting as a crypto growth hacker and longevity researcher, hopping from conference to conference and speaking on stages around the globe. But deep down, I couldn't shake this feeling that something was off.

You know, that little voice in your head, that gnawing feeling in your gut. It felt like a cold acid pumping through my veins. I could feel it move throughout my entire body. It would snake its way through my stomach, through my neck, and then to my arms. I would wake up in a cold sweat in the middle of the night. It would give me headaches and make me sick with mystery illnesses. The doctors said, "Oh, it's normal. Probably just stress." At the time, neither the doctors nor I had any idea that a Netflix thriller was in the making right under my nose.

The dreams that woke me up in the middle of the night told me things. They told me of the devastation that would ensue. Deep down, my subconscious brain recognized patterns of things that seemed off, but I didn't seem to register them when I was conscious and awake. Not yet. I knew something felt off, but I couldn't quite put the puzzle together. I'm not even sure I knew it was a puzzle at the time.

The Netflix thriller would grow into a series, with many episodes and years like this. The cold acid kept pumping. It ran through my veins so thick and almost stopped me dead in my tracks. I kept silencing the sensations in my body and didn't know exactly what could be wrong. I only knew it felt incongruent. Something was amiss. But what?

I was busy living life, after all. Great career, and on the face of it all, it seemed like a happy marriage. I was close to my family and friends, living and working from a sailboat on the Greek island of Syros. Why wouldn't I be happy? Why would I question my life?

I've always had a good dose of skepticism and a healthy relationship with reality; yet for some reason, these signals weren't entirely registering to my conscious, awake mind. My body felt them much before my mind caught up.

Ever done that? Want to believe in the best of a situation or a person? Yeah, me too.

What I didn't realize at the time was that my gut instincts weren't just random or dramatic, as I was told. They were my body's way of urgently trying to warn me that something was wrong. My subconscious mind knew, yet my conscious brain was protecting me from not knowing and registering all that was happening.

Those off feelings were red flags waving from my subconscious mind, urgently trying to break through my daily grind. At the time, I dismissed those gnawing sensations as overthinking, stress, too much caffeine, or a bad day. I was also convinced daily that these were the reasons. When someone you love is reassuring you constantly, naturally, you want to believe them.

There's a scientific fact you need to know, one that your grandparents and parents probably already told you: your gut instincts are never wrong. They will never deceive you. Ever.

If you ever get an off feeling about a person or a situation, you need to know to pause, slow down, and not be in a hurry to make any decisions. Rarely will you ever regret pumping the brakes. In the next few pages, I will be sharing a story about how an investor was saved from investing $8M in a fraudulent venture.

In our professional lives, we set out to grow our companies to a certain level. We start with organic growth and then consider partnerships and acquisitions. Sometimes we get so focused on our mission that we don't tune in to our intuition. We rely only on logic and then wonder how we make bad business decisions involving our clients or investors. This happens all the time, not just in business but also with our health and our relationships.

Why? Because more often than not, we're in a hurry, and we don't take the time to be still, quiet, and intentionally tune into our intuition. Quick snap decisions can often turn into costly regrets.

Looking back and after years of training as a neuroscientist in an effort to understand others, it led me on a journey into a whole new universe and a different approach to service—one with more purpose and meaning to me.

Gut feelings aren't random. They are signals. They are part of a rapid-fire communication system between the brain and the gut, one that operates at lightning speed, in microseconds, long before we consciously process what's happening. Most of us are completely unaware of this.

This system, known as the gut-brain axis, is one of the most fascinating things I've ever researched. It's a two-way communication highway connecting your brain and your gut through the vagus nerve and other pathways in our bodies. Think of it as your internal internet. Your vagus nerve is your AI. It's more powerful and smarter than you ever realized. When you learn how to optimize it, it's like you possess a secret weapon in your business, health, and all relationships.

Your gut processes what's happening in your environment, sometimes even before you're fully aware of it and sends those insights to your brain and back to your body. That's where those feelings in your gut come from. But sometimes the communication system has a poor signal, and things aren't clear. There are a multitude of reasons why this can happen. We'll get to that in the coming pages and how to optimize and fine-tune your signals.

That sinking feeling in your stomach is not just in your head. It's your gut speaking directly to you, urging you to pay attention. But will you listen?

Here's what's wild: this communication between your gut and your brain happens in microseconds, faster than your conscious mind can analyze a situation. It's like your body's built-in early warning system, designed to keep you safe, make better decisions, and avoid potential harm. But here's the catch. It only works if you know how to read it, feel it, and if you're listening and know how to respond to it in a way that benefits you.

I love biohacking as it can be the best on-ramp to longevity, healthspan, and joyspan for anyone. One of the primary biohacks I love the most is around optimizing your intuition. Why? Because it guides everything in your life. After all, life is all about choices.

There are mountains of research and evidence-based studies on the vagus nerve, gut-brain access, and the subconscious mind. I help you understand this, apply my protocols, and leverage the gut-brain axis to understand and use it to your advantage. And like any skill, it can be developed, refined, and trusted. My mission is to help you understand it from a neuroscience perspective, in a way that you can apply it in your life today.

So let this be your wake-up call. Your gut is speaking. Are you listening?

I became fascinated with the science of intuition from a neuroscience perspective based on my journey. And in my research, both evidence-based and anecdotally, I discovered countless stories of people having gut instincts that stopped them in their tracks and made them take immediate action to prevent them from doing something or to encourage them toward doing something. And for many others, they heard and felt the gut instincts but didn't act. For many, something devastating, often tragic, happened, as in my case.

And for the ones who did pause, listen, and act in accordance to what their gut instincts were screaming at them to do, I discovered countless stories of people cheating death, avoiding horrible accidents, outcomes, or having it put them on a path that changed the trajectory of their lives for generations to come. This kept me in awe. I wanted to understand how instinctively some listen and some don't. I wanted to understand how that affects people's lives in their business, health, and relationships as I experienced my upheaval after a tsunami, so this became personal.

Many of the people I interviewed for my book, *Inner Code: The Science and Secret Wisdom of Intuition*, have gone on to make profound scientific discoveries, see massive growth in their companies, creating both impact and scale at a mass level.

Others have started companies that are changing the world in longevity science. Even though they were told it would never be possible, some people, against all odds, followed their gut instincts to start families despite a devastating accident or health crisis. Story after story, we see extraordinary people expanding their impact and legacy. Why? Because they listened to their gut instinct. So it got me thinking, what if I could teach more people how to read their intuition, trust it, and act upon it in accordance with those feelings? Would we create and birth more Leonardo da Vincis? Bob Dylans? Elon Musks? Sara Blakelys? Kobe Bryants? Taylor Swifts? More Buck Institutes for Research on Aging? More Dr. Deb Riveras? More Peter Diamandises? More Dr. Rosalind Franklins? More Loreen Wales? More Leila Hormozis? More Arianna Huffingtons? More Oprahs? More Simone Bileses? People who have and are currently changing the world and impacting the countless lives of others. You get the picture.

What made some listen to their intuition, while others don't actually understand what I mean when I say that? Was it because some of us got a second chance and therefore we were going to create something impactful in this world? Or was it the trauma that led to the transformation? What exactly was it?

This fascinated me and sent me down a rabbit hole, insatiably curious to research it all. You see, I didn't start out as a biohacker, neuroscientist, or longevity researcher. In fact, I used to think that I got here by accident.

I quickly came to see that everything that happened, as horrific as it was, was a gift.

A divine redirection from the Universe.

What is the "why" behind what you do?

My calling is important to me because everything up to this point brought me to where I am today, right here with you, on a path of true purpose and meaning to serve.

We have never been more curious as a human species about how we operate. If we don't believe this, look at the phenomenon of *The Dr. Andrew Huberman Lab Podcast*, the beloved and wildly successful podcast host and professor of neurobiology at the Stanford University School of Medicine. He is the #1 rated podcast in science, education, and health. Never before has so much information been accessible to us, and now we want to understand it all and how it applies to our lives.

That's what led me to share this with you regarding the science of intuition, as it's not something talked about much, and it impacts our lives greatly—every single day.

As a fellow entrepreneur and human with a packed schedule much like yours, I understand that you're all faced with decisions each day, some big and some small. You have the capacity to change the trajectory of your life and impact your reach and growth in your business, health, and relationships, maybe in ways you've never yet thought about.

That's why I wrote this chapter, and my next book, to remind you that your intuition is your best biohacking secret weapon in life. It lives within you. It's free. And most of us don't pay enough attention to it. But if you did, it could change your life in the most profound ways.

Most of us don't know how to tune into our intuition. It's not something we're ever taught. And really, most don't think of how to biohack it. On top of that, most of the world is still unaware of the vagus nerve in our bodies or even that the gut and the brain are an interconnected two-way communication system. The microbiome in your gut? Guess what? They talk and send signals to your brain.

The vagus nerve is like your body's secret communication superhighway, connecting your brain to your heart, gut, and other vital organs. It plays a key role in regulating stress, digestion, heart rate, and overall balance. When it's activated through deep breathing, meditation, or even humming, it signals your body to shift from fight-or-flight mode into rest and digest mode, promoting calm, focus, and healing. For entrepreneurs, learning to harness the vagus nerve can improve mental clarity, boost resilience, and prevent running on empty for too long. This makes your vagus nerve an essential tool to know how to leverage for high performance.

Most of us are not taught about our nervous system. What could that have to do with your business, health, or relationships? It turns out everything. Your vagus nerve is interconnected to the part of the nervous system responsible for involuntary control over breathing, heart rate, and digestion. This is unbeknownst to most people. Right now, it's working for you, and you don't even need to tell it to. It just happens automatically. That's why it often gets ignored.

It's also the nerve that interconnects through the gut and the brain axis to give you those butterfly or gut feelings in your body when something feels exciting or something feels like it's going horribly wrong.

My mission is to help educate, provide access, and democratize the fact that biohacking, longevity, healthspan, and joyspan are for all of us.

Consider this fact: a private longevity doctor costs approximately $100k per year, and then there are the medications, supplements, treatments, injections, etc. If someone can afford that and wants to go that route, I believe everyone should do what makes them happy. But I also hear a lot of criticism in our space that only the rich and elite have access to longevity and a greater healthspan. I am here to tell you that is untrue. It all begins with access to information, education, and knowing what to look for.

What I teach you in this chapter is an introduction to my work, and it's accessible and free to everyone.

The Gut Feeling and Your Senses:

So how would you rate your intuition? Would you say you're good at reading people? Situations? Bosses? A merger or acquisition opportunity? A romantic life partner? A fling? Can you walk into a room and read the energy quickly? Can you decode body language easily?

Would you say that you have a calm lifestyle with stable patterns? Or would you say you have a tendency to attract the wrong people and things into your life? Are you often surrounded by bad luck or chaotic situations? This is how you do an audit of your life. Look back at the choices you made regarding your business, health, and relationships. See the patterns. How did your intuition stack up?

When I'm working with CEOs, corporate sales teams, executive leaders, blockchain foundations, musicians, Olympic athletes, doctors, scientists, and entrepreneurs, I apply my BRAINS Model™ (six ways of thinking) to do an audit of their past decisions, both positive and negative and why they worked or didn't.

The ultimate goal is to review how you make decisions. Most of us lean heavily to one area over the other in the BRAINS Model. This exercise is intended to have you consider all aspects of the BRAINS Model. Did you make decisions relying solely on logic, for example? Or did you blend intuition and the six ways of thinking? Most executives and top performers do the numerical and analytical thinking quite well. It is often reported to me that they skip the rest. Take out a notebook and pen or use your voice recorder on your phone to do this exercise and do an audit of your last ten big decisions.

BRAINS Model™

- **B**: **Big-Picture Thinking** (Strategic): Aligning with long-term goals
- **R**: **Reflective Thinking**: Checking alignment with your purpose
- **A**: **Adaptive Thinking**: Flexibility and creativity in the moment
- **I**: **Insight Thinking**: Listening to your gut and intuition
- **N**: **Numerical Thinking** (Analytical): Crunching the data
- **S**: **Social Thinking** (Empathetic): Considering team and customer impacts

I encourage the clients I work with to keep a journal of their decision-making. You will become more aware of the decision-making patterns in your life. Take a look into your past. The patterns will emerge. You will see them clearly.

Don't get discouraged if your audit isn't looking good. It's a wonderful opportunity to make a shift in your life. And if so far your track record is pretty good, congratulations. Even if we make a 1% shift, for you, these are the biggest shifts that can change the trajectory of your life.

So, why weren't we taught this as children or in school, you may ask? No one is to blame, per se. In general society, school, parents, and work all reward logic and data-driven thinking over feelings. It's that simple. That's why intuition has taken a back seat in modern society and is often overlooked. But when you are not skilled at this, it can cost you dearly.

Interestingly, ancient wisdom has always known about intuitive-based decision-making long before we had neuroscience. Today, fMRI brain scans and heaps of evidence-based data prove to us that the gut-brain axis and vagus nerve connection is our intuitive guide in decision-making.

Few children or adults today are taught what intuition is, how to read it, and how to communicate it to their parents, caretakers, and teachers. It also requires having parents, caretakers, and teachers who know about it. So you can see why most of us are not skilled in this practice, and it gets easily overlooked.

When you know how to read your intuition, it's like learning a new language. It opens up a whole new world of opportunities. It's why certain executives reach the C-suite and become CEOs, millionaires, and billionaires.

It's why some successful and well-known, self-made entrepreneurs, like Leila Hormozi, CEO of Aquisition.com, listened to her gut instincts when she realized an investment she was about to make with a potential business partner didn't feel right. She talks about being really close to signing an $8M real estate investment deal with this person. And as she got further along in the deal-making process, she noticed something didn't feel right.

The first question she asked herself was, "Does this person share the same business values with me?" And the answer was an easy no.

She talks about having seen a few moments where the person had said or done certain things that raised some red flags for her. At the last minute, even though all her friends and colleagues were still a part of the deal, she pulled out.

Leila said her gut told her it was not the right investment with the right person. Eight months later that person was indicted for fraud, and all her friends lost 100% of their multimillion dollar investments.

Leila avoided losing an $8M investment. That's the power of understanding your intuition, learning to tune in, and making sound business decisions based on it. What made her know while everyone else did not? This is a common occurrence, to miss the signs. She is credited with saying that her values guided her even more than her intuition. She was clear on her values. Again, this is something most of us don't take the time to get clear on. When you know your top five core foundational values, this can be a powerful guidance in your business, health, and relationships.

Anyone can do it. It takes practice and daily repetition to become fluent in reading your intuition. It also helps you read and understand others much better and with great empathy. You become a better leader with much sought after soft skills when you use your EQ, IQ, and solid intuition to make deals and decisions—skills that AI can't replace.

Since we're talking about neuroscience, stories we tell ourselves and how we frame things in our mind, I'm going to ask you some questions to get your mind working beyond reading.

Our Senses

How many senses do you think we have? You think the answer is five, right? [sight, touch, taste, smell and hearing].

Well, guess what? The answer is you have thirty-three senses.

Why am I talking about this when I was just telling you about gut instincts? Because it's all interconnected. These thirty-three senses are part of our sophisticated communication network. That's how much power you have access to within your body.

Biohacking and neuroscience go together. They're besties. Because the point of biohacking is to create quick wins (i.e., release dopamine) to motivate you to want to continue to pursue them more often.

Learning and consistently doing hard things are the best biohacks for rewiring your brain for resilience, focus, and ultimately, the proven results you've been looking for to tap into your intuition. Here's the good news: you are not hardwired. You are not stuck with any version of yourself that you wish to change. You can change your mindset, body, and outlook at any time in life. It's one of the greatest longevity biohacks there is, and just knowing that you have that choice is an immensely powerful fuel. I encourage you to use it.

When and why did you decide to become an entrepreneur?

After a tsunami nearly took me under, it didn't take long for me to see everything so clearly. Things zoomed into perspective quickly. I completely re-evaluated my life and did an exercise on listing out my core values. Eventually, I narrowed it down until I got to five core foundational values. Every decision I made needed to pass through my core foundational values.

I knew I no longer wanted to be working for any companies or crypto projects whose core values didn't align with mine. I was not interested in launching a project in a foreign jurisdiction that would involve deceiving people or lead to nefarious activities. Other than knowing how to make other people money, I knew I had a new purpose

I knew I was going to pour my life force energy into serving others in a way that felt more meaningful and transformative to me. I felt like I knew a secret, and I wanted to share it with anyone who was interested in learning more.

I started my company called *Proof of Good* because of my journey. I stopped trading my time for someone else's dream. Beyond getting rich, I doubt the places I previously worked at even knew their dreams or their *why*. It was a case of the blind leading the blind. This happens more often than not. Ever have a boss or a board of directors you didn't vibe with? It usually has something to do with a misalignment in core foundational values. It always goes a lot deeper than a personality conflict.

How were you able to transform a setback into a setup for success?

I chose purpose and meaning. I chose to honor karmic beliefs, trusting that every action carried a ripple effect and that my response to pain could create something meaningful in the world to help others. Instead of succumbing to resentment, I embraced the idea that what we give to the world, whether it's love, forgiveness, or purpose, inevitably shapes our journey. This perspective became a guiding principle, transforming suffering into an opportunity for growth and service. I knew I wanted to serve differently than I had in the past, which was primarily focused on making companies and start-ups a lot of money. There's nothing wrong with that, but sometimes I think people can get so focused on one thing that they lose sight of the big picture.

What unique framework or service do you offer to your community or clients?

I have several frameworks and protocols at Proof of Good. For this chapter, I chose to share my BioHack Stack Method™ to help you get started in firing up your intuition to make transformative changes in your business, health, and relationships. It's also a healthy tool to rebalance your hormones, digestive track, and feelings of overall well-being.

My Framework: The BioHack Stack Method

I created the BioHack Stack Method to simplify the path to optimization:

- **S** – Spark: Identify what inspires you
- **T** – Transmit: Share your energy and intention
- **A** – Activate: Take action aligned with your values
- **C** – Chemistry: Balance your hormones and biology
- **K** – Knowledge: Continuously learn and adapt

Your Brain Needs Proof

Your brain plays a key role in biohacking, particularly through your reticular activating system (RAS). This system is constantly working to confirm and prioritize what you're thinking about. That's why I often ask people to keep in mind statements like "I have imposter syndrome," "I'm not a morning person," or "I'm not a good public speaker." This is because when you repeatedly think or say these things, your brain will find proof to confirm that they're true. That's neuroscience, not woo. Be careful how you talk to yourself.

Your brain is constantly performing value tagging, categorizing, and prioritizing the thoughts and beliefs you've told yourself are true or important, even if they aren't. With your brain, it's all about efficiency, helping you focus on what it perceives will keep you safe and alive. The catch? Your brain doesn't know it's the 21st century. Yes, it knows the date. But the deep part of your brain, the amygdala, the part of the brain responsible for fear and survival instincts, still operates as if you're living in a cave, unless you train it otherwise.

With biohacking, proof is essential here; your brain needs measurable results to stay motivated. Seeing progress creates a positive feedback loop, reinforcing your effort and commitment to change. Whether in business, health, or relationships, proof validates authenticity and trust. Similarly, your brain requires proof—those small wins—to commit to biohacking or any new habit.

By aligning your actions with good intentions and measurable outcomes, you create ripples of positive impact, both internally and externally.

What's your favorite biohack and why?

Let's do one hard thing together: water fasting. It's free, powerful, and accessible to everyone. Water fasting involves drinking only water (and black coffee/tea) for a set period. It redirects your life force energy from digestion to healing and transformation. Most people will be surprised to learn that our bodies naturally make an Ozempic, which is a GLP-1. Make it for free, and your body will thank you.

Start with an 18-hour fast and build up to 24, 36, and then 72 hours. The benefits are profound: increased energy, mental clarity, hormonal balance, growth of stem cells, and a natural testosterone boost for both men and women. The scientists who have inspired me the most in the science and fields of fasting are Dr. Valter Longo and Dr. Alan Goldhamer.

But here's something you might not expect: fasting fine-tunes your intuition. Scientifically speaking, fasting shifts your body into a state called ketosis, where your brain runs on ketones instead of glucose. Ketones are a cleaner and more efficient energy source, leading to enhanced mental clarity and focus. Meanwhile, the gut-brain axis, the communication highway between your digestive system and your brain, becomes less distracted by digestion, amplifying your ability to notice subtle signals from your body and environment. This heightened state of awareness can feel like your intuition turning up its volume, helping you make clearer, faster, and more confident decisions.

When you remove distractions like constant eating, you create space to listen to your body, your thoughts, and those subtle gut feelings that are always there but often drowned out. Water fasting helps you tune into this internal wisdom, sharpening the connection between your brain and body in a way that's both grounded in science and deeply empowering.

How can people connect with you?

I can be found on LinkedIn @Jawna Standish and in our Longevity & Enthusiasts Telegram community at: https://t.me/+HF7ag3o2v5o0Y2Nh

BIOHACKING ISN'T JUST ABOUT OPTIMIZATION; IT'S ABOUT LIBERATION FROM THE PATTERNS THAT HOLD US BACK AND THE METRICS THAT DON'T SERVE US.

Andrea Wanerstrand

CHAPTER 11

FROM PRADA HEELS TO MUCK BOOTS
BY ANDREA WANERSTRAND

From the outside, my life was a stereotypical picture of success. I had a beautiful family, a large house in an "it" neighborhood in the city, and a thriving career in the corporate world, climbing the ranks at T-Mobile, Hitachi Consulting, and Microsoft. Every year, we took vacations to Hawaii, creating memories that looked perfect on the surface. My days were filled with high-stakes meetings, polished presentations, and a steady stream of accolades.

Yet behind the scenes, I was crumbling. My health was suffering across the board: insomnia plagued me nightly, high blood pressure was becoming a norm, and I had significant weight gain. I developed allergies to gluten and alcohol, was constantly getting sick, and felt perpetually exhausted. My life, which read like a textbook for corporate success, was a veneer hiding my reality.

Despite my outward accomplishments, I felt unfulfilled and disconnected from the vibrant energy

I once had. The turning point came when I could no longer ignore the warning signs: the doctor blatantly told me test results that were "*not* good." My worries and fears were mastering me. That night, when insomnia kept me awake at 2 a.m., and with a body screaming for change, I had a moment of sleepless clarity. I made a commitment to myself to get healthy—physically and mentally. But where to start? Inspired by the innovation of tech hackathons, I applied the same approach to my life: breaking problems into manageable parts, creating actionable solutions, and rebuilding myself with the same analytical rigor I once reserved for work.

That decision set me on a quest for biohacking—a transformative journey to optimize my mind and body.

I didn't leap straight into the unknown, though. As I began exploring this new world, I remained tethered to corporate life, experimenting within the safety of my role. At Microsoft, I drew inspiration from Satya Nadella's push to transition from a "know-it-all" to a "learn-it-all" culture. His words unlocked something I had long suppressed: beneath the layers of corporate polish, I was an entrepreneur at heart, yearning to build something uniquely my own.

Determined to test this realization, I started small. I spearheaded internal initiatives, developed coaching programs for sales teams, and crafted strategies to foster growth mindset principles within leadership. Each project was a mini-hackathon, fueled by curiosity and the desire to innovate. I gravitated deeper toward coaching, helping peers navigate career transitions, promotions, and leadership challenges. It wasn't just work; it was exhilarating.

By 2018, I transitioned to Microsoft's Learning and Development team, where I designed and launched a coaching capability program for leaders. The initiative exploded across a hundred countries, impacting tens of thousands of employees. The feedback was extraordinary, and leaders began seeking me out for personal coaching. This work felt deeply meaningful, but the seeds of entrepreneurship had taken root. My desire to create something outside the confines of corporate life grew stronger by the day.

The defining moment came on a rainy Tuesday in Seattle. I stood in front of a room full of executives, presenting the results of my coaching program. The metrics were impressive—massive engagement, cultural shifts across the organization—but the real impact lay in the stories of personal transformation. As I spoke, I felt an unmistakable clarity. This wasn't just another meeting; it was a crossroads. While some leaders grumbled about investing in "soft" skills, several others saw the immense value that behavior change brought to both business outcomes and people's lives. These executives approached me, asking if I would coach them personally. I knew instantly that these were the people I wanted to work with—leaders who understood the transformative power of mindset and were ready to make real, lasting change. It was then I knew my corporate chapter was nearing its end.

Shortly after, I traded PowerPoints for biohacking journals and BI dashboards for wearable tech. I left the corporate world to focus on building something new—a life that prioritized health, fulfillment, and meaningful impact. But this transformation wasn't just about leaving one world behind; it was about rediscovering myself.

I found refuge on a lavender farm on a small island, not far from the noise and constant demands of the city. I traded in my Prada heels for muck boots and learned to drive a tractor. There, surrounded by the ebb and flow of the sea and the calming scent of lavender, I began to listen to my thoughts—really listen. On the island, there are no takeout deliveries or instant gratification. If I want something, I plan for it. I have to be intentional about when I hop the ferry and invite the noise of the city back in. Without distractions, I had to confront the ways I had tied my worth to external markers like job titles and paychecks. The stillness was humbling, but it gave me the space to redefine success.

While owning and running the lavender farm has been an important part of my healing and grounding process, it's just one of my businesses. My primary focus is on Mindset Maven Method™, where I coach high performers—corporate leaders, entrepreneurs, and creators—to break free from cycles of stress and unlock their full potential with as little friction as possible. Rooted in my belief that "what worries you, masters you," I help my clients optimize their mental and physical energy, boost productivity, and develop unshakable confidence to reach their goals at any stage of life or career. I show them that they can achieve both financial prosperity and wellness of mind, body, and spirit. Today, I'm healthier and more fulfilled than I ever was in my six-figure corporate career—and yes, I make more money too.

The key to healing your life is to heal the beliefs that hold you prisoner. I stopped saying yes to things that didn't align with my values. I stopped living on autopilot, constantly waiting for the next weekend or vacation to escape. Instead, I built a life rooted in intentionality and aligned with my deepest priorities.

This clarity became the foundation of my entrepreneurial journey. As a biohacking entrepreneur, I merge the analytical precision honed in corporate boardrooms with the relentless curiosity of a growth mindset. I work with clients to unlock their full potential, blending neuroscience, physiology, and mindset practices to drive sustainable transformation.

Biohacking isn't just about optimization; it's about liberation from the patterns that hold us back and the metrics that don't serve us. My mission is to help others redefine success on their terms and live a life of purpose, connection, and vitality.

Entrepreneurship, I've learned, isn't about leaving structure behind; it's about alchemizing the best of what you've learned into something new. My journey—from corporate success to a lavender farm, from leadership coach to biohacking entrepreneur—is proof of what's possible when you approach life with curiosity and intention.

And to think it all began with a sleepless night, a commitment to myself, and a decision to hold a hackathon on my life.

What is the "why" behind what you do?
I have always been driven by the belief that work environments can and should be places where people thrive—not just survive. I founded A3 Culture Lab, LLC to help organizations, from start-ups to multinational corporations, build human-centric cultures one leader and one team at a time that foster authenticity, autonomy, and accountability. I have seen firsthand that what the highest performers have in common is they have learned how to show up consistently, owning their authentic presence with emotional intelligence. They have learned to be comfortable owning their autonomy in deciding their path, and they consistently hold themselves accountable, owning the good, the bad, and the messy.

My journey hasn't been without its challenges. Like many of the leaders I coach, I've faced burnout and the constant juggling act of career, family, and personal well-being. It's what led me to embrace resilience, biohacking, and mindset mastery as core components of personal development. I firmly believe that "what worries you, masters you," and my mission is to help others break free from that cycle and unlock their full potential with as little stress as possible.

What unique framework or service do you offer to your community or clients?

The Mindset Maven Method™: Harnessing Thought & Energy for Maximum Impact & Minimum Stress

The Mindset Maven Method™ is a transformative system I created to help business leaders and entrepreneurs develop the mental, emotional, and physical energy skills necessary to eliminate burnout and reduce the micro stressors to thrive, adapt, and stay motivated in achieving their goals both at work and at play. This framework blends *science and self-discovery*, drawing inspiration from the ancient art of *alchemy*—the process of turning base elements into gold. Just as alchemists sought transformation and refinement, this framework guides individuals to transmute thoughts, emotions, and energy into growth, resilience, and high performance.

Grounded in the latest neuroscience and enriched by my experience working with high-performing teams, the Mindset Maven Method™ offers a holistic approach to personal development. It taps into the *mind-body connection*, leveraging the power of emotional awareness, mindset shifts, energy level management, productivity hacks, and sustained habit formation. By embracing both *logical strategy and intuitive growth*, this framework reflects the essence of alchemy—blending the tangible and the intangible to create profound, lasting change.

The goal is not only to help individuals think in new ways but to foster *continuous transformation* by experimenting, refining, and aligning mental and physical energy with personal and professional aspirations. In doing so, business leaders and entrepreneurs can unlock maximum impact in their lives and careers, experiencing deeper fulfillment and heightened performance.

Four Pillars of the Framework

Pillar 1: Emotional Awareness and Alignment

What it is: This pillar is all about helping you notice things you might not be aware of (blind spots) and making sure your personal values match your work/life goals. Most of our thoughts and emotions—about 95%—exist in our subconscious. This means that becoming aware of the mind-body connection and paying attention to the signals our body gives us is critical for emotional awareness.

Why it matters: When your goals match what you care about, you feel more focused and motivated. Recognizing the physical and emotional signals from your body allows you to align your actions with your deeper values and needs.

Sample Actions:

- **Reflection Time:** Take ten minutes at the end of each week to write down what went well and what felt challenging. Look for patterns. Pay attention not only to what you thought about but also how your body felt, what emotions you experienced, and your energy levels throughout the week. This helps you understand the mind-body connection and develop emotional awareness.

- **Values Check:** Write down your top five values (like honesty, growth, or creativity) and ask yourself if your current job or project supports these values. If not, consider what minor changes could be helpful.
- **Body Scan Exercise:** Set aside five minutes daily to sit quietly and scan your body from head to toe. Notice any areas of tension or discomfort. Reflect on the emotions tied to those physical sensations.
- **Emotion Tracking:** Keep a journal to track your emotions throughout the day. Write down moments when you feel stressed, happy, or anxious. Look for patterns in how your emotions shift.
- **Breathing Exercises:** Practice deep breathing for five minutes each day to help calm your nervous system and increase awareness of how your body responds to stress.

Pillar 2: Growth Mindset Activation

What it is: This pillar helps you develop a growth mindset, which means believing that you can improve by learning and trying new things, even if it feels hard at first.

Why it matters: When you believe you can get better, you're more likely to take on challenges and learn from mistakes.

Sample Actions:

- **Reframe Mistakes:** The next time something doesn't go as planned, write down one or two things you learned from the experience instead of focusing on what went wrong.
- **Try Something New:** Pick one new skill or activity to try each month. It could be as simple as learning a new app or speaking up in a meeting.
- **Embrace Feedback:** Actively seek feedback in areas you want to improve. Choose one piece of feedback to implement immediately, and track your progress over the next month.
- **Challenge Assumptions:** When faced with a difficult task, ask yourself if you are holding any limiting beliefs. Write down an alternative perspective and take action based on that.
- **Visualize Success:** Spend five minutes each day visualizing yourself succeeding at a new task or goal. This can boost confidence and improve performance over time.

Pillar 3: Energetic Alignment and Vibration Management

What it is: This pillar emphasizes managing your body's energy levels and the vibe you project to those around you. Energy isn't just about physical stamina; it's about the frequency you emit and how it influences your environment and interactions.

Why it matters: Your energy influences your moods, productivity, and level of motivation. Additionally, it is always a factor in how others perceive you and how effectively you lead or collaborate. High-vibrational energy fosters positivity, connection, and inspiration, while low energy can hinder progress and drain those around you.

Sample Actions:

- **Daily Energy Audit:** Rate your energy levels at different points during the day. Note when you feel the most vibrant and when you feel drained. Adjust your schedule to align important tasks with high-energy periods.
- **Movement and Flow:** Engage in movement practices like yoga, tai chi, or dance to cultivate energy flow throughout your body.
- **Environmental Scan:** Regularly assess the environments you spend time in. Remove clutter, add natural elements, and ensure your space feels energetically supportive.
- **Intentional Connection:** Before meetings or social interactions, take a moment to ground yourself and set an intention for the energy you want to bring.
- **Nature Immersion:** Spend time in nature to recharge and harmonize your energy.

Pillar 4: Habit Stacking for Increased Productivity & Sustained Momentum

What it is: This pillar focuses on maintaining progress by linking new habits to existing ones. Habit stacking is a simple yet powerful way to make positive behaviors part of your daily routine. By anchoring small, beneficial actions to habits you already perform, you reduce decision fatigue and create a foundation for consistent productivity and stress reduction.

Why it matters: Building consistency is key to long-term growth. By attaching new habits to established ones, you can seamlessly integrate personal development into your life. This method not only ensures follow-through but also minimizes the overwhelm by making new tasks feel familiar and manageable. Research by James Clear, author of *Atomic Habits*, shows that high performers leverage habit stacking to automate success and sustain momentum over time. Clear emphasizes that "success is the product of daily habits—not once-in-a-lifetime transformations."

Sample Actions:

- **Morning Journaling (2 min):** Upon awakening and while brewing your morning coffee or tea, spend two minutes journaling your goals or intentions for the day.
  Productivity Hack: Keep your journal next to the coffee maker or on your nightstand. This physical cue reduces the barrier to starting.

Let your thoughts flow naturally. There is no need for a structured to-do list; just focus on how you want to show up in the world. **High Performer Insight:** Tim Ferriss, author of *The 4-Hour Workweek*, integrates morning journaling with his coffee routine to prime his mind for clarity and creative problem-solving.

- **Post-Meeting Reflection (5 min):** Immediately after each meeting, take five minutes to reflect on key takeaways and note one actionable step.

  Productivity Hack: Pair this with updating your calendar or task manager. This habit prevents miscommunication, solidifies insights, and reduces the stress of forgotten details.

  High Performer Insight: Sheryl Sandberg, former COO of Meta, habitually follows up meetings with written reflections, reinforcing clarity and action.

- **Gratitude Practice (3 min):** At the end of the day, after shutting down your devices, write down three things you are grateful for.

  Productivity Hack: Link this with brushing your teeth or setting your alarm. A calm and grateful mind lowers stress, promotes restful sleep, and enhances focus for the next day. **High Performer Insight:** Oprah Winfrey incorporates gratitude practices before bed, linking it with winding down for a more peaceful evening.

- **Accountability Partner (1 min):** While having your morning coffee or during your lunch break, send a quick message to your accountability partner about your daily progress.
  Productivity Hack: Automate reminders on your phone or pair this with scrolling social media. Engaging with someone else adds a layer of motivation and external reinforcement.
  High Performer Insight: Athletes like Serena Williams check in with coaches or mentors daily to stay accountable and maintain peak performance.
- **Movement Breaks (2–5 min):** After every hour of sitting, stand up, stretch, or take a quick walk around your space.
  Productivity Hack: Link this with refilling your water bottle or switching tasks. Short, intentional breaks reduce fatigue, enhance circulation, and refresh your mind, leading to sharper focus and less burnout.
  High Performer Insight: Tony Robbins schedules movement breaks during work sprints to stay energized and boost productivity throughout the day.

Bonus Habit Stack Ideas:
- **Mindfulness Minutes:** After turning off your morning alarm, take three deep breaths before getting out of bed.

- **Learn While You Move:** Listen to podcasts or audiobooks while exercising or during commutes.
- **Hydration Habit:** Drink a glass of water immediately after brushing your teeth.

By incorporating these small but powerful hacks into your daily routine, you'll amplify productivity, reduce stress, and create sustainable habits that contribute to long-term personal and professional growth.

The application of integrating all four of the pillars of Mindset Maven Method™ is backed by science and techniques that empower individuals to harmonize their thoughts, emotions, and energy. Research in neuroscience and psychology demonstrated that emotional awareness (Feldman Barrett, 2017), growth mindset (Dweck, 2006), energy regulation (Frederickson, 2009), and habit formation (Clear, 2018) significantly enhance performance and resilience. This interconnected system amplifies impact and cultivates authenticity, allowing individuals to show up consistently in both mind and body as their best selves in all areas of life.

What is your favorite biohack and why?

Many biohacks require expensive technology or equipment, but there is one simple and powerful biohack that doesn't cost a thing—meditation. Meditation is not just about relaxing; it's actually a science-backed way to improve how your brain works. And guess what? Meditation isn't about clearing your mind or sitting in total silence. There are many types of meditation; the key is to hack until you find the type that fits you. It's a chance to understand your mind and body better. Meditation helps you notice your thoughts and feelings, and with practice, you can improve them.

How Meditation Changes Your Brain and Body

Studies show that regular meditation can actually change your brain in helpful ways. Scientists have found that meditation strengthens parts of your brain that help with memory, learning, and emotions, like the hippocampus and prefrontal cortex (Luders et al., 2009). It can also shrink the part of your brain that controls fear and stress, called the amygdala (Taren et al., 2013). This means meditation can help you feel calmer and more in control.

Dr. Joe Dispenza, a meditation expert, explains how meditation helps rewire your brain. He says it helps break bad habits and negative thinking by creating new, better pathways in your brain. This can lead to big changes in how you feel and act.

Physical Benefits of Meditation

Meditation isn't just good for your brain—it's good for your body too. Regular meditation can lower your blood pressure, reduce inflammation, and boost your immune system (Black et al., 2015). Dr. Dispenza's research also shows that meditation can change your body on a cellular level, helping you stay healthier and more energized.

Meditation and Peak Performance

Meditation also improves focus and self-awareness, skills that are critical for top performers. When you meditate, you train your brain to stay on task and ignore distractions. This helps you reach a flow state, where your productivity and creativity are at the peak. Meditation also helps you understand and manage your emotions, recognize your strengths and weaknesses, and stay calm under pressure. This state is called "coherence," where your brain and heart work together in harmony. This makes it easier to perform at your best, whether you're working, learning, or dealing with tough situations.

By practicing meditation, you can build these same skills, making it easier to stay cool and collected, even during stressful times (Brewer et al., 2011).Overall, meditation can help you feel healthier, think clearly, and handle whatever life throws your way.

A Simple Guide to Meditation

If you're ready to give meditation a try, here's a simple guide to get you started:

1. **Find a quiet place** where no one will bother you.
2. **Sit comfortably** with your back straight and your hands on your knees.
3. **Close your eyes** and take a deep breath in through your nose. You should feel the breath all the way in your stomach. So *really* deep. Hold it for a few seconds.

4. **Exhale slowly** through your mouth. Do this a few times.
5. **Pay attention to your breath.** If your mind wanders, take note of your thoughts, then just gently bring your mind back to your breathing.
6. **Keep doing this for about five minutes**. Over time, build up to fifteen to twenty minutes.

How Meditation Has Helped Me

For years, I struggled with insomnia and felt drained of energy during the day. I would toss and turn at night, and no matter how much I tried to rest, I woke up feeling tired and foggy. This lack of quality sleep made it hard to focus and left me feeling exhausted.

When I started practicing meditation regularly, everything began to shift. Meditation helped me calm my racing mind at night, which made it easier to fall asleep and stay asleep. Over time, I noticed my energy levels during the day improved, and I felt more mentally sharp and physically balanced. On the days when I skip my meditation practice, I can clearly feel the difference — my mind feels more cluttered, and I feel more tired and less patient.

Incorporating meditation into my daily routine has not only improved my sleep, but also boosted my ability to manage stress and stay focused throughout the day. It has become my go-to biohacking tool that helps my journey to be a better leader, a prosperous entrepreneur, and live a healthier, happier life.

How can people connect with you?

I can be found at https://a3culturelab.com and on LinkedIn at www.linkedin.com/in/andreawanerstrand

CONCLUSION

You made it to the end of this book, but your journey is just beginning.

By now, you've read the stories of entrepreneurs who have transformed their health, mindset, and businesses through biohacking. You've seen how small, intentional changes can lead to increased energy, sharper focus, and greater resilience. More importantly, you've been given the tools to implement these strategies in your life.

The question now is, what will you do with this knowledge?

Because information alone doesn't create transformation, action does.

The Choice Is Yours

Entrepreneurship is demanding. It will test you in ways you never imagined. But here's the truth. The greatest investment you can make isn't in your business. It's in *yourself*.

If there's one thing we hope you take away from this book, prioritizing your health isn't separate from your success. It is the foundation of it.

You don't need to implement every strategy at once. Start with one. Make it a habit. Then stack another. Over time, these small adjustments will create a ripple effect in every area of your life and business.

Final Lessons to Carry With You

- **You are your greatest asset.** Treat your body and mind like they are the most valuable parts of your business—because they are.
- **Energy is currency.** Guard it. Invest in it. Optimize it.
- **You don't have to accept burnout as the price of success.** There is another way.
- **Experiment and stay open.** The best biohack is the one that works for *you*.
- **Your success is directly tied to your well-being.** The better you feel, the better you perform.

Where Do You Go From Here?

This is not the end. It's a starting point. You now have the knowledge, inspiration, and roadmap to take control of your health, your performance, and your future.

We encourage you to take action, share what you've learned, and explore new ways to optimize your life. The greatest version of you is waiting.

We can't wait to see what you create.

To your health, success, and impact,

Wendi Blum Weiss & Patricia Wooster

ABOUT THE AUTHORS

WENDI BLUM WEISS

Wendi is the founder of The Speakers and Coaches Networking Society, an international audience of 18K+, where she provides education, resources, and support to help hundreds of purpose-driven entrepreneurs amplify their voices, reach more people, and elevate their impact.

Also, a podcast host, published author of seven books, and an international speaker, she has spoken on college campuses, taught courses around the world, led international retreats, and hosted masterminds on topics that combine elevating your energy and harnessing your brilliance as it pertains to creativity, productivity, health optimization, and business success.

In 2022, Wendi joined forces with Patricia Wooster to empower entrepreneurs to stand out in a crowded marketplace by building their audience, community, and brand through becoming bestselling authors, speaking on stages, and evolving their brand into a trusted authority.

Together, they combine the best of entrepreneurial wisdom, energy tools, and community to help more people unleash their greatness both personally and professionally.

PATRICIA WOOSTER

Patricia is the founder of WoosterMedia Publishing, where she helps experts, executives, and entrepreneurs codify their wisdom and leverage their expertise into books, digital courses, workshops, speeches, consulting, and media opportunities. Her clients include C-level executives, college professors, professional athletes, and media personalities who have landed agents, major publishing contracts, speaking opportunities, and bestseller status.

ABOUT THE AUTHORS

She is the author of nineteen books, including the award-winning and bestselling *Ignite Your Spark* with Simon & Schuster, and three entrepreneur co-author books with Wendi Blum Weiss. Her experience ranges from working with companies and organizations like Disney, Home Shopping Network, WeDay, Informix Software, Designing Genius, and KPMG to working with start-up entrepreneurs and influencers.

Today, she is partnered with Wendi Blum Weiss to teach entrepreneurs how to successfully brand themselves as bestselling authors, speakers, and experts in their field.

In addition to helping people unleash their superpowers, Patricia and Wendi are passionate about teaching entrepreneurs how to leverage their energy through functional health practices and the newest biohacking protocols to increase performance and creativity. They believe the key to a purpose-driven life is optimizing physical vitality and mindfulness, empowering entrepreneurs to establish themselves as influential thought leaders while prioritizing their well-being.

LEAVE A REVIEW

Before you go, if you enjoyed this book, will you please consider leaving a review on Amazon? As authors, there is nothing we appreciate more than reading reviews on Amazon and other bookseller websites from those who have enjoyed the book.

Thank you so much!
Wendi Blum Weiss & Patricia Wooster

Made in the USA
Columbia, SC
02 April 2025